Sue Price has been involved in children's ministry
1984. She is currently on the PCC and is involved
Beans (toddler group) and Sunday school (for a few jannnns ...
Sue is author of 100 Simple Bible Craft Ideas, Children's Ministry Guide to
Working with Under 5s, *and* Children's Ministry Guide to Tailored Teaching
for 5–9s. *She is editor and contributor to* TotZone Year 1—God is so Big, TotZone
Year 2—Thank You God, *and was concept creator and editor of Y-Zone, KidZone*
and MiniZone curriculum for children aged 3–12 from 1999 to 2008. Sue has been
Director of the Children's Ministry Conference since 1998. She is a well-known seminar
speaker and workshop leader in various aspects of children's ministry.

Ruth Alliston has been involved in children's ministry for over 40 years in the Salvation
Army, house churches and NFI, teaching Sunday school and organising holiday clubs and
camps. Ruth is author of Children's Ministry Guide to Storytelling *and* Children's
Ministry Guide to Using Dance and Drama, *and was creative contributor and writer*
for KidZone and MiniZone curriculum for children aged 3–9 from 1999 to 2008. She
is a seminar speaker and workshop leader in various aspects of children's ministry and
grandmother to ten grandchildren ranging in age from 4 to 15.

Barnabas for Children

Barnabas for Children® is a registered word mark and the logo is a registered device mark of The Bible Reading Fellowship.
Text copyright © Sue Price and Ruth Alliston 2012
The authors assert the moral right
to be identified as the authors of this work

Published by
The Bible Reading Fellowship
15 The Chambers, Vineyard
Abingdon OX14 3FE
United Kingdom
Tel: +44 (0)1865 319700
Email: enquiries@brf.org.uk
Website: www.brf.org.uk
BRF is a Registered Charity

ISBN 978 1 84101 880 5

First published 2012
10 9 8 7 6 5 4 3 2 1 0
All rights reserved

Acknowledgments
Unless otherwise stated, scripture quotations are taken from the Contemporary English Version © American Bible Society 1991, 1992, 1995. Used by permission/Anglicisations © British and Foreign Bible Society 1997. American Bible Society 1997.

Scripture quotations taken from the Holy Bible, New International Version, copyright © 1973, 1978, 1984 by International Bible Society. Used by permission of Hodder & Stoughton Publishers, a member of the Hachette Livre UK Group. All rights reserved. 'NIV' is a registered trademark of International Bible Society. UK trademark number 1448790.

The paper used in the production of this publication was supplied by mills that source their raw materials from sustainably managed forests. Soy-based inks were used in its printing and the laminate film is biodegradable.

A catalogue record for this book is available from the British Library

Printed in Singapore by Craft Print International Ltd

Few Children
Great Opportunities

12 stand-alone sessions for mixed-age
church-based groups

SUE PRICE AND
RUTH ALLISTON

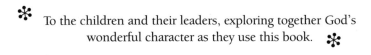 To the children and their leaders, exploring together God's
wonderful character as they use this book.

Contents

✳

Foreword

Some years ago, I was with Sue and Ruth on a stand showcasing children's work resources. We were unable to meet one person's request for what she wanted to occupy her group—colouring sheets. Despite our efforts to show her the value of more creative activities, she was adamant: colouring sheets were all that were needed! Now, colouring sheets have their place... somewhere. But surely our children deserve more than that!

Working with Sue and Ruth over many years has opened my eyes to the multitude of ways in which children discover Jesus and respond to his love, and thus the importance of giving them a range of experiences and learning opportunities. I have found Sue and Ruth to be the most practical of visionaries. They are passionate in promoting quality and creativity in children's ministry, with each child valued as unique and precious to God. At the same time, they understand the challenges facing children's workers and parents, and have always aimed to do all they can to make the role as fulfilling and enjoyable as possible.

This book is a treasure trove for all who struggle to provide meaningful times for small and fluctuating groups. It is an inspired concept, whereby sessions can be experienced in any order or no order and still be relevant and fun for both children and leaders. What a bonus, at a time when the importance of faith in the family is rightly being highlighted, to have ideas to follow the themes through the week in the home!

... And never again will I see a white van without shouting out 'Joy'!

Catherine Kyte
Faith Support Officer, Mothers' Union

✳

Introduction

Few Children, Great Opportunities is designed for church groups with very small numbers and a mixed age range from 3 to 11 years. That doesn't mean the material isn't appropriate for larger groups or a single age group. It just means that there are no assumptions about the levels of physical, mental or emotional maturity that the children may have reached and there are no team games or activities that require large numbers—no more than a child and two adults (to comply with your church child protection policy).

This book doesn't ask why you only have a small number of children in your group. It may be a result of the demographic of your community, there may be another, more family-focused church in the locality, or you may have large numbers of children attending other programmes in the church. Other books, such as *Messy Church* (Barnabas, 2006) and *Not Sunday, Not School* (Barnabas, 2006), give strategies to develop alternative events for families and children but, however successful fresh expressions may become, they often do little to increase the number of families attending the traditional Sunday service. Yet there are still some families who want to come along regularly or occasionally on a Sunday morning, and the church needs to provide for them.

If this is your situation, you will probably already have tried several methods of dealing with small groups or irregular numbers of children with a wide age range, and have discovered that there is no 'one size fits all' solution. How much easier it would be if there were! A traditional teaching programme or other published resources will generally need considerable adaptation, and a leader who spends time preparing thoroughly may find that there is only one child one week, three the next, and perhaps none the next time. Any children who do come may be of disparate ages, making it even more challenging to prepare in advance. Naturally, many leaders become despondent and less willing to devote the time and energy needed to prepare well.

Sporadic attendance isn't only a problem for churches with small numbers of children. In any church, a child may attend on alternate weeks because they are visiting Dad, who now lives some distance away, on the other weeks; a family may come only occasionally, when everyone gets up and ready on time; visits to family and friends, holidays, football matches and shopping trips all result in weeks missed. If you are using sequential material, a child can quickly lose the thread that is running through the series of sessions. When your group is small, however, sporadic attendance is magnified and leaders will be more aware of the issue. If three children don't come when you have 15 on the register, it makes little difference to the leader, but, if there are only those three on the register, it is another week when the leader has prepared pointlessly. This is a particular problem if you are following a sequence of sessions and have a rota of leaders, as holding over a prepared session can mean that it is used out of context later.

So the requirement is for a resource that is thematic rather than sequential (sessions can be used in any order, yet still build on each other, so that the programme doesn't just consist of random Bible stories that are never set in context for the children), is suitable for a small number of children with a wide age range, and can be modified at the point of delivery to be appropriate for the children who are present.

We aim to bring a fresh and encouraging look at how a small group of children and adults can learn together about God. It's also important for children to know and understand that, while they may be doing something different from the rest of the church at a given time, they are very much part of the church, both local and universal. We want to foster the sense of belonging to God and to each other, and help children come to love him and want to respond.

The person preparing the sessions doesn't need to be a Bible expert; we refer to that person as the facilitator. The material is structured to offer learning opportunities from Jesus and the stories of other people and organisations, and then to consider how the group and the individuals in it—adult facilitators, helpers and children—might want to respond. Churches obviously need to be sure that they are adhering to appropriate child protection policies, with at least two adults working with the children, and they may also choose to have facilitators who are trained in aspects of children's ministry and who regularly meet for Bible study. However, teenage helpers or older children could be invited to prepare and facilitate part or all of a session. This approach also means that the material can easily be used by children's cell groups.

Because a small number of children with a mixed age range also defines many families, the content can be adapted for home use by families who want to spend time growing in faith together. Some churches are successfully attracting new families to monthly programmes such as Messy Church, but they don't have the resources to increase the frequency of the event. Each of the twelve sessions in this book could provide material for families to explore together at home over the course of a month. This option is covered in more detail in the section headed 'Using the material at home' (see page 24).

The sessions in this book concentrate on the character of God. Scripture tells us that 'the only one who truly knows the Father' is the Son, but that 'the Son wants to tell others about the Father, so that they can know him too' (Matthew 11:27). None of us can wholly know the unknowable God, but through his word and through his Son we can begin to know him and have the rest of our time and eternity to discover more of his wonderful character and nature. When we begin to know and appreciate who God is, we can begin to worship him and honour him with our lives. We want both adults and children together to be formed and shaped in the character of God and to explore his life in and through them.

- Each session is themed, and it doesn't matter in which order the sessions are used. In your initial preparation you may wish to discuss with your church leader the preaching programme for the coming few months and see if any of the sessions are more appropriate for particular weeks. Once prepared, however, a facilitator can hold a session over and use it at any later date if no children turn up.

- Each session is flexible and can be easily adapted to the time available, whether 20 minutes or over an hour. If you only have a short session time, the material can be shaped into two or more sessions so that you are not wasting material. See the section headed 'Adjusting the material for shorter sessions' (p. 22).

- Emphasis is given to forming and growing a relationship with God and the people around us, and learning to serve God and each other.

- Much of the preparation for the session by the facilitator will consist of reading the Bible references, thinking through their own responses and becoming familiar with the options and ideas suggested.

- The activities suggested, together with various options, can be customised to the numbers and ages of the group, even adapting at the point of delivery. It may sometimes happen that all the items prepared do not get used on a particular day. This shouldn't be regarded as a waste of time or effort, as these items can often be used or adapted on another occasion, and will save preparation time later on.

- Each session includes ideas for home follow-up that can be suggested to parents, but the whole session can also be adapted to be used at home by families who want to set aside a time to connect with God and each other. See the section headed 'Using the material at home'.

- Positive attention is given to developing an awareness of the mystery and wonder of God and finding meaningful ways together to celebrate him and express love for him.

- Everyone is encouraged to:
  * discover God's character through the actions or teaching of Jesus.
  * find out how people have responded to God in the past (both people in the Bible and in more recent history).
  * discover people and organisations today who are responding to God through love and action.
  * consider their own response.

Heads, hands and hearts

We tend to think that it is detrimental to the children if they are in a group with a wide age range because we can't tailor the Bible teaching to their developmental level. But several commentators in the area of children's ministry and spiritual development have recently challenged this belief.

In particular, in her book on children's spirituality, Rebecca Nye writes:

To improve the child-friendliness of their work with children, churches emulate the age-divided, age-appropriate approach to intellectual development that is followed by schools...

Learning information and being able to turn ideas round is often well served by this developmentally sensitive approach. But it is not inevitable that spirituality is subject to the same restrictions. There's a real danger here of making the error of over-identifying spirituality and intellectual ability. We need to take seriously the alternative—that spirituality might have less to do with age, intellect and mental life, and much more to do with being and feeling.

REBECCA NYE, *CHILDREN'S SPIRITUALITY* (CHURCH HOUSE PUBLISHING, 2009), P. 84.

The Church of England report *Going for Growth: transformation for children, young people and the Church* challenges the church to try to become the good news rather than just teaching the good news. It points out:

Christianity teaches that all human beings are made in the image of God (Genesis 1:26–27). This means that all people whether they are four months, six, 15 or 90 years old, are complete human beings. Our problem, as human beings, is that we are clear from our experience that we are born as infants and then grow and develop gradually into adulthood. But this perspective, which drives so much of our education, law, social behaviour, parenting and relationships towards children and young people, distracts us from a fundamental truth about human existence, which is that God does not view us exclusively in this way and does not judge us on how old, wise or developed or 'finished' we are.

This material seeks to offer a balance between discovery—of something about God's character and of stories about people through history who have striven to behave in a godly way—and engagement, through the opportunity to worship, consider a personal response and grow spiritually. Both discovery and engagement are reinforced by giving children the opportunity to be active and use as many of their senses as possible.

In the sessions, we use the following symbols:

- 😊 growing head knowledge through storytelling
- ✋ supporting knowledge by activity
- ♡ developing heart knowledge

You will find choices in each of the sections that will help you tailor the material for your time and group, but we would encourage you to ensure that you have a balance of head, hand and heart elements in each session.

Story and activity

Ivy Beckwith says:

I began to think that one of the ways, if not the way, children develop faith and are spiritually formed is through having their imagination captured for the kingdom of God…

It would seem that if our faith has any credence at all then the idea of living in the kingdom of God must have some compelling pull to it. After all, the New Testament is full of stories of people literally dropping everything to follow Jesus. And the history of the church is full of the same kind of stories of people being compelled to give up wealth, careers, and life in order to work in and for the kingdom of God. So what must it take to capture our children's imaginations, and then souls, through the hope and magnificent love of God's kingdom? …

It takes being intentional with story, ritual, and relationship at home, in the faith community, and in worship with children.

IVY BECKWITH, *FORMATIONAL CHILDREN'S MINISTRY* (BAKER BOOKS, 2010), PP. 14–15

Capturing a child's imagination has little to do with their chronological age. You will, of course, need to take account of children's ages as you choose the vocabulary you use for your stories and discussions, or as you think about the dexterity required for an activity. It is important to tell stories in a way that the youngest children present can understand (you can use questions to check that they have grasped the key points and retell parts of the story if necessary) but don't discount all activities or ideas that may seem too old or too young for the children present. Older children are often happy to participate in an activity that seems 'simple' and, if they do not have to put all their effort into concentrating on the task, you can also engage them in a conversation about the theme. Conversely, if an activity seems too complex for a younger child, it is often possible to find a simpler level for the same idea or provide assistance.

It's fine to bring toys for younger children if you have a fairly long session. The toys may be related to the theme, but not necessarily. Small children can't concentrate for as long as older children and will usually play happily for a while as older children complete an activity or do something else. Younger ones can be invited to join in again later.

Ritual

In *Few Children, Great Opportunities* we develop a story book as a focus or ritual that enables a record of Bible stories to be built up and reviewed, acts as a prayer diary and becomes a communal journal for the small group of children. Everyone can contribute to the story book and then they can look back, discovering the chronology of the Bible, recalling stories already heard and seeing how they fit in with the current story, and praising God for answered prayers. Children can proudly show the story book to other members of the church family, and leaders can use it to keep track of the sessions taught and children's attendance.

Children, especially younger children and those with autistic spectrum disorders, are comforted by familiar routine and the church has long known that ritual can bind a faith community together. Many of you will belong to churches where the ritual of the liturgy is important and where different liturgical colours are used to mark the church seasons.

We follow the same structure for each session while varying the activity ideas, enabling you to establish a familiar, not boring, routine. We have also used colour as an additional way of recalling the twelve characteristics of God that we explore in this book. Older children who can read and understand how an index works may be able to find the story of Jesus being tested in the desert (Luke 4:1–13) in the story book, but all children can find the black pages used for the session about self-control. Then, later, when they see a blank black screen at home, they may remember that they can show self-control by not constantly asking to watch a DVD or TV programme or play a computer game.

Wondering and open-ended questions

Our aim is to bring our groups before God, learning, worshipping and playing with and alongside each other, and experiencing the awe of being in the presence of Almighty God. This is a journey of discovery for all concerned, both adults and children. We want to reclaim the art of thinking, contemplating and being gently guided to find our own answers in God. As Rebecca Nye says, 'Habitual wondering about spiritual matters, and in response to spiritual content (such as Bible stories), inspires children to value the possibility that fresh insights might be yielded each time, as opposed to things being fixed once and for all' (*Children's Spirituality*, p. 38).

The material in this book uses wondering and open-ended questions, which help to make it appropriate for a wide age range. But, as we introduce the concept of open-ended questions, we also bear in mind that children (especially younger children) may be 'concrete learners', finding it difficult to engage in abstract imagination. Those of you familiar with the techniques of Godly Play will know how it uses the precise placement of objects to encourage children to wonder about a story. The sessions in this book are not so prescriptive but they do encourage the use of familiar objects to help children to start thinking.

You may have one or two young teens in the congregation who sometimes want to come out with the children. Or, if the material is being used in a home setting, there may be a mix of ages that includes teenagers. The open-ended questions will enable them to respond at their own level of understanding. If appropriate, remind them that the group is for the children but you'd be happy to carry on the conversation afterwards. Encourage them to sometimes take responsibility for preparing all or part of a session.

Facilitators should take time to think about their own responses as they prepare, and should be ready to provide answers to questions, to ensure that the teaching has been understood. Adults, though, can be too ready to fill a silence. Children need time to process a question and you should be prepared to leave a silence of up to a minute after making a wondering statement. Sometimes you may then give your own response, but you may choose to move on. Just because a child doesn't verbalise a response, it doesn't mean they haven't thought it through and grown spiritually as a result.

✳

Getting the best out of the material

We have talked about the flexibility of the material, but, as you start to prepare, you will know the approximate length of time available for your session. Also (subject to occasional surprises), you will be aware of the possible numbers and ages of children who are likely to come along, though not necessarily the exact combination that will be present on the day. This section will help you to select and prepare the material that is most likely to be appropriate for the time you have and the children you may expect, while giving you options to adjust on the day.

One of the advantages of having only a small number of children in your group is that you have the opportunity to get to know them and their families well, and this will help you to shape sessions that make the experience deeper and sharper for everyone concerned.

Planning and recording

If you have more than one person responsible for preparing sessions, it is important that you come together to plan, pray for the children and support each other. There is no need to take the sessions in the order they are presented in the book. You may wish to liaise with the church leaders: if there are any Bible passages or themes in common with the preaching programme over the coming weeks, these might influence the order in which you use the material.

Although the sessions stand alone, they are linked by the common theme of discovering something of the character of God, and it is helpful if connections are made between the sessions. To do that effectively, facilitators need to know what has already been covered and which children were present. The story book is key in enabling this to happen. Each week, in the index and register section of the story book, the facilitator should record the session information and the children present. This makes it easier to be relevant to each child as you use the review element in a session.

📖 The story book

Your story book will be best as a loose-leaf folder (bought or made) but could be a large scrapbook or even a special box. Craft shops sell different kinds of paper, whose colours and textures will add pleasure and interest. We use colour as an aide-memoire for each of the different characteristics of God explored in the material, and creating pages for your story book in the appropriate colours will help children to find and recall previous sessions.

The story book needs to be divided into four main sections: an index and register at the front, a prayer diary, a Bible story section (which will gradually need to have Bible book dividers added), and an 'Our stories' section where you can record information that children research on historical characters, Christian organisations and their own responses to the session themes.

In each session, suggestions are given as to what might be included in the story book but children should be encouraged to make their own creative contributions. At the end of a session, older children, a teenage or adult helper or the facilitator can look up a Bible index to check the right order to file the Bible story and its associated creations. Photographs can be added, for example, of crafts that the children want to take home or service acts being carried out.

Index and register

This section enables all leaders to see what has been covered and which children were present, so it can be helpful as you look back to review sessions and prayer requests. Each week you should record the date, facilitator's name, session title, Bible passages covered and children present. Here's an example of what an entry in your index and register might look like:

16 October   Facilitator: Sue
God is kind   John 6:1–15 (feeding 5000)
                      Ruth 2 (Boaz and Ruth)
Children: Molly, Thomas, Josh, Heidi

This is also an appropriate place to record any food allergies and so on that any of the children suffer, so that leaders are reminded to take them into account as they plan activities.

Prayer diary

This section can be used to record, in date order, any specific issues that the children ask to be included in your prayer time. It will generally be easier if an adult or teenage helper records the prayer and the name of the child making the request as it is raised. The helper can also look back over past weeks and ask the children if previous prayers have been answered, enabling the group to praise God for his answer and recording the response in the story book.

Bible stories

As Bible stories are covered in sessions, they can be entered in the 'Bible story' section in Bible book order. This helps the children to understand how the Bible fits together and can place one story into context with another from a previous session. As an example, you might use the following stories:

- God is trustworthy: 1 Samuel 1:1–28 (Hannah)
- God is kind: Ruth 2 (Ruth and Boaz)
- God is powerful: 1 Samuel 17:1–50 (David and Goliath)

David was Ruth's grandson and was anointed king by Hannah's son, Samuel. Older children will really enjoy understanding these timelines and history.

Our stories

The final section can be used to record the stories of historical characters and Christian organisations that are researched as part of a session. You could also include information and pictures of any response activities that you plan and carry out.

You might want to consider making an online version of the story book for your church website, scanning appropriate pages and adding links to other websites, especially if you are encouraging families to follow up on the sessions at home.

Session content

Each of the twelve sessions has the same structure:

- Way in
- Learn from Jesus
- Time to praise God
- Discover other people's stories
- Respond
- Review
- Way out

There is also a family follow-up section at the end, giving ideas for activities that you could encourage families to do together at home.

If you have a session that lasts 45 minutes or longer, you will probably want to keep to the structure as presented, selecting from the various options in each element. If your time is shorter, we give you some alternative ideas in the section below on adjusting the material for shorter sessions.

Although many of the activities engage multiple senses and include elements of 'head', 'hands' and 'heart', we indicate the main element for key sections to help you ensure that you include a balance of activities.

Way in

Each session starts with objects that relate to the theme or story in some way. These objects help to focus attention on the topic in a very concrete way, which is particularly important for younger children. They are used as a conversation starter to connect with the theme but they may also be used later in the session or revisited in the 'Way out' section at the end. You may like to have a special bag or box that you bring out at the start of every session, building the mystery or excitement of discovering the particular objects for the week.

Each session explores an aspect of God's character and each aspect has a colour associated with it. We suggest that you place the objects on a sheet of appropriately coloured paper, perhaps to be used as a page in the story book later on, or a piece of coloured material. This introduces the colour from the very beginning of the session. Dedicated facilitators and helpers could also choose to wear appropriately coloured clothing.

Learn from Jesus

The main Bible teaching for each session is a passage from the Gospels where we discover something of God's character from the actions or teaching of Jesus.

In each session we provide you with several ways to tell the Bible story. The ages and preferred learning styles of your group of children will influence your choice. If you might only have older children present, especially if they are fluent readers, you could opt to have a child-friendly Bible (such as the International Children's Bible or the Good News Bible) with you to use. After telling the story, you can use questions to check that the children have understood the story, and 'wondering' to set them thinking deeper.

Children learn best when they interact with the story. One or more activities that will help them explore the story are included, at least one of which is appropriate to be included in the story book. Specific materials that you will need are listed, but it is assumed that you will have standard craft materials available each time, such as paper of different colour and textures, felt-tipped pens, crayons, scissors, glue, sticky tape, sticky tack and so on.

Time to praise God

It may be difficult to include singing if you only have one or two children. We include some simple songs, rhymes and chants to fit the theme of each session, but you may prefer to use songs that are familiar and favourites. 'Galatian fruits' by Ishmael would be a good theme song for the series (available on the CD *52 Scripture Songs*, Kingsway Music, and as a download from the Kingsway website). If you are not sure whether you will have younger or older children present, have a couple of different CDs available, offering songs they can sing along with. We would recommend Ishmael or Julia Plaut CDs for younger children and Duggie Dug Dug or Hillsongs CDs for older children. Duggie Dug Dug's *Funky Action Songs* DVD (Kingsway Music) includes actions and dancing with the songs. Children of all ages may prefer to join in with the actions rather than singing.

Some children may not want to participate in singing at all. We give alternative activities for non-music worship and we also include a Bible memory verse activity.

Discover other people's stories

The main Bible story for each session shows the character of God through the life of Jesus. In this section of the session, we give options for exploring people from the Bible and from more recent history who have attempted to reflect God's character in their own lives. Younger children can empathise with the behaviour of a person in a simple story and children of all ages will find stories a helpful way to make sense of the abstract godly characteristic that you are exploring.

Depending on the time you have available, and the interests and abilities of the children present, you may choose to use one or more of the stories. We provide a story for one character in each session and general activity ideas that you can use to follow up all the story options. We also identify a national organisation that has a ministry reflecting the godly characteristic addressed.

Many churches will have connections with national or local organisations or will support people serving God in particular ways at home and abroad. You can use their stories and links to make the sessions even more relevant to your children. Because most organisations and individuals will display several of the godly characteristics covered in this book, it would be a good idea for all the leaders to work together at the planning stage to allocate your local connections to appropriate sessions.

Providing information about, or giving older children the way to research, organisations or individuals will encourage everyone to feel that they are part of the universal church, working with and supporting each other. It may also help to spark responses in the next section of the session.

If you have a long session time, you may want to include a time of free play for younger children, whether or not you have older children present. If you have access to a wide range of toys suitable for under-fives, we suggest a theme that connects with the session but that isn't essential.

Respond

The *Going for Growth* report by the Church of England says, 'We are called to work towards the establishment of the kingdom of God here on earth and our engagement with children and young people must reflect the values of the kingdom… It should call us to work with and equip children and young people to challenge oppression and injustice' (p. 9).

If we are to move beyond just telling Bible stories, it is important to give children the opportunity to respond to the session in ways that reflect their spiritual maturity and their age-related physical abilities. Listen to children's ideas, share your own if appropriate, and help to shape some practical possibilities.

This section also includes time to pray. Each session gives ideas for prayers that relate to the theme, based on the simple model of thanking God, confessing our sins and asking for his help. The benefit of having a small group and knowing the children and their families is that you can take the opportunity and time to pray in specific ways, relevant to the children's current experiences. Record specific prayer requests in the story book.

It may be helpful to have a soft seating area for discussion and prayer times. It can be created with large cushions, blankets, beanbags and so on.

Review

Review answers to previous prayers. Check where today's Bible story or stories fit into your story book and look at how they relate to other stories that you've previously studied. Recall and review some of the things you learnt and planned to do as a result of studying those stories. File today's story book activities in the right places.

Way out

Each session ends with a final brief activity, which will often link back to the 'Way in' object or activity.

Family follow-up

If you have a small number of children in your church, it is likely that all the children from each family will be in your only group. At the end of each session we provide ideas that you can give to the families to encourage them to think about the character of God at home together. The ideas are divided into four sections: Play, Praise, Plan and Pray. The Play activities can be done as a family together or by children individually, with or without parental assistance. The Praise, Plan and Pray sections are more appropriate for families to use together at one time or in several short bursts during the week.

You will need to give information to families on the Bible verse and stories you have discovered in your session, plus details enabling them to find out about the other people or organisations that you didn't cover.

Families that enjoy craft activities could work together to create a 'God is…' collage, patchwork, embroidery or something similar over the period, adding the twelve characteristics as they are covered.

You can download 'Family follow-up' sheets to customise and print or email, from www.barnabasinchurches.org.uk/extra-resources/.

Adjusting the material for shorter sessions

Obviously you will choose how to truncate the material if there is too much for your session time, but the temptation is to think that the Bible story is the most important element and to cut all the opportunities to reflect and grow spiritually.

There are several ways to spread the material over more than one week to get the full benefit of the various elements, and here we give you two ideas. The first splits the session into two, and will still give you enough ideas for sessions that last up to 30 minutes or longer if you have mainly older children. The second is for groups that have a very short time with their children, possibly only 15 minutes, and it splits each session into three or four.

Using a session over two weeks

We suggest that you plan to have the same facilitator for both sessions. That way, the facilitator knows exactly what was covered in the first week and can build on it in the second session. Also, if there are no children present in the first week, the facilitator can hold the material over and use it when they are next on the rota. Ideally, the two sessions will be taught consecutively, but that isn't essential. Split the elements as below.

Week One

- Way in
- 🙂 🖐 Learn from Jesus
- 💚 Time to praise God: Select activities to match the time you have. You may also want to include a time of prayer
- With older children and to extend beyond 30 minutes: Discover other people's stories (use a historical or contemporary character or organisation option)
- Way out: Include time to file your story book activities

Week Two

- Review: Place your story book on your coloured cloth or paper and review the 'Learn from Jesus' story from the first week. How you do this will depend on whether you have the same children, different children or a mixture.
- 🙂 🖐 Discover other people's stories (choose one of the Bible stories and an activity)
- 💚 Time to praise God (select activities to match the time you have)
- With older children and to extend beyond 30 minutes: Use another option from 'Discover other people's stories'
- 💚 Respond (include time to file your story book activities)

Using a session over three or four weeks

Ideally, the three or four sessions will be used consecutively and sequentially if you have very short sessions, as you won't have the time to set each week into the context of the whole theme.

Week One

- Way in
- Learn from Jesus
- Way out (include time to file your story book activities)

Weeks Two and Three (or just Week Two)

- Review: Start by quickly reviewing the 'Learn from Jesus' story from the first week in your story book

- Discover other people's stories: Choose one of the stories and an activity
- Praise God: Select activities to match the time you have and allow time to pray and file your story book activities

Week Four (or Week Three)

- Review: Start by reviewing your story book, particularly the stories from the first three weeks
- Respond: Add a 'Praise' activity if you have time

Using the material at home

A small number of children with a mixed age range describes many families, so this material is ideal for use by families who want to spend time growing in faith together. The 'Family follow-up' section gives ideas to extend each session at home, but some churches may be looking for stand-alone resources that they can give or recommend to families to explore together at home.

The material can readily be adapted to be used at home over the course of a year. It doesn't require a leader with detailed Bible knowledge, so it can be used by any family, but the church leadership team may wish to ensure that family facilitators can turn to someone in church with any questions that may arise. This is especially relevant if families have only recently entered the church community and it is known that the adults have no more grounding in the Bible or Christian faith than their children.

We would recommend that each session is taken as the family focus for a month and that the contents are divided in a similar way to our suggestion for using the material over four weeks in church. This gives a core of material that families can explore together for about 15 minutes each week, but then the associated activities can be carried out throughout the week by individual family members, or in groups, or all together. The creation of a story book can become an important focus for family Bible discovery and spiritual development as well as growing into a wonderful heirloom.

If you want to be very organised, you can plan for the material to last for 48 weeks, rather than twelve months, slotting in two weeks exploring Christmas and another two weeks looking at the Easter story.

✳

God is love

- **Theme:** We can spread Jesus' love
- **Learn from Jesus:** Matthew 5:43–48
- **Bible verse:** 'Dear friends, let us love one another, for love comes from God' (1 John 4:7, NIV).
- **Discover other people's stories:** Jonathan; Moses' family; C.T. Studd; Thomas Barnardo; WEC
- **Theme colour:** Red

Way in

Spreading stickiness

Bring: Red paper or cloth; slices of bread; butter or margarine; strawberry or raspberry jam; plastic knives; plates; wipes; plastic film

Cover a table with red paper or a red cloth.

Say: I wonder why we are using the colour red today…

Put the food items on the table.

Say: I wonder what we could do with all these things…

Listen and affirm ideas without comment. Help everyone make jam sandwiches.

Say: It's good to have things that spread easily. Stickiness spreads everywhere, too!

Have everyone wipe their fingers. Cover and save sandwiches to be eaten at the end of the session.

Learn from Jesus

Matthew 5:43–48: Today's story is about when Jesus told people to love everyone. People watched Jesus doing things and spreading God's love wherever he went. They told their friends about him, and their friends came to watch Jesus and listen to him.

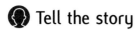 Tell the story

Choose the story option most appropriate for your group.

Jesus spread God's love everywhere he went. Everyone knew about Jesus. Everyone wanted to be near him and feel God's love. They heard Jesus talk about God's love. One day, people followed Jesus all the way up into the high hills.

Jesus sat down and the people sat down too, as close as they could. Jesus said, 'You know how it is—when someone hurts you, you want to hurt them back. But God wants you to be loving, like him. Not just loving to your own family and your best friends. That's the easy bit! God wants you to be loving even when people are unkind or hurt you, or don't love you back. God wants you to be loving, like him, and spread his love, like I do.'

1. Follow my leader

Have the children follow a leader slowly around the room, down a corridor, up stairs or outside if suitable. Lead and walk as you start telling the story, then sit down together for the rest of the story.

2. Watch my face

Read the story sentence by sentence. Children can make up actions for each one. Appoint a confident reader to be Jesus, while listeners choose expressive faces as an accompaniment to Jesus' teaching. Put the whole drama together.

3. Find the story in the Bible

An adult or child may read Matthew 5:43–48 from a Bible or children's Bible storybook, such as *Barnabas Children's Bible*, No. 262.

Consider the story

- I wonder why people wanted to be near Jesus…
- I wonder what we would have thought if we had been there…
- What did we find out about Jesus in that story?
- In what ways does Jesus spread God's love? How can we do that, too?

Explore the story

Choose one or more activities, depending on your group and time.

 ### 1. Spreading red

Bring: Kitchen roll; saucers; red food colouring; water

Say: What's today's colour? Red is often used as a colour for love.

Pour a little red food colouring on to a saucer for each person. Add water. Everyone can fold a sheet of kitchen roll into four and place it in their saucer, turning it over until it has absorbed as much water as possible and is covered all over.

Say: See how love has spread all over the paper. It's spread on to our fingers, too!

Leave the paper to dry. Later, when it's dry, you may cut out a heart shape and write 'God is love' on it.

 Stick a 'God is love' heart in your story book.

2. Salted!

Bring: Packets of different flavoured crisps, including one salted and one unsalted variety; bowls

Put the crisps in separate bowls without letting the children see the packets. Invite them to identify the different flavours.

Say: Which crisps are salty? Which crisps aren't? Salt mixed with food makes it tasty and enjoyable. We need a little salt each day to keep us healthy.

Point out the salted varieties.

Say: The salt is spread right through these crisps. Whoever we share these crisps with gets some salt. God wants his love to spread right through us so that we can share it with others.

 Stick an empty, salt-flavoured crisp packet in your story book, writing, 'When we follow God's ways, we will be like a little salt in the cooking pot, making the whole meal taste good.'

3. Follow God's ways

Illustrate the sentence 'When we follow God's ways, we will be like a little salt in the cooking pot, making the whole meal taste good' using three pictures: footprints with a signpost showing 'God's ways'; a cooking pot over a fire; someone with a full tummy and a big smile.

Stick the pictures in your story book.

♡ Time to praise God

Hold up a Bible. Explain that the Bible story told us that Jesus spread God's love wherever he went. Jesus shows us what God is like. God is love.

It tells us in the Bible

Dear friends, let us love one another, for love comes from God. (1 John 4:7)

> **Bring:** Envelopes or postcards; stamps (optional)

Find and read the Bible verse. Explain that this is part of a letter from John to other Christians. John was Jesus' best-loved friend. Older children can write out the verse like a letter, writing John's name at the end. You can write or print out the letter for younger children and they can decorate a border around it.

Options: Put the letter in envelopes and post them to your church leaders; display them on a church notice board; take them home to display; stick them in your story book.

Music praise

You can sing together or along with a CD or DVD. Some children may prefer to do actions, dance or jump around rather than sing. Alternatively, you can play a CD while doing the Bible verse activity. Choose songs relating to God's love (see page 19 for suggested CDs).

Activity options

1. Spread all over us

Bring: Duvet; shopping catalogue

Say: Do you have a duvet or blankets at home?

Show children the duvet section in the shopping catalogue, with the duvets in their packets.

Say: Duvets are bought all tightly wrapped in shiny plastic—impossible to sleep under. What do we need to do to sleep under a duvet?

Sit on the floor, spreading the duvet over everyone. Repeat each line with a clapping rhythm for children to copy:

God is always loving.
His love is ever the same.
Always there for us.
Spread all over us.
God wants us to spread his love
Till everyone is covered.

2. Pass it on

Bring: Red paper hearts; plastic beakers

Fix a heart to the bottom of a plastic beaker for each person. Sit in a circle or, if there are only two of you, opposite each other. Everyone holds a beaker in their right hand so that the heart is on the top. Say the sentence below slowly, moving your beaker from right hand to left hand and then on to the person on your left, as follows: 'I can praise God for his love…' (move beaker from right to left hand) 'and I can pass it on…' (pass beaker to person on your left).

Start slowly, saying the sentence together and moving the beaker from right to left. Repeat, moving beakers in rhythm and passing them on each time, gradually getting faster until the game collapses.

Discover other people's stories

Choose from the options below to discover people who were (or are) inspired to be loving, like God.

 Tell their story and discuss how they show God's love through their actions.

- Jonathan: a loving best friend to David. Find the story below.
- Moses' family: risked their own lives to save the life of baby Moses. Find the story in your Bible (Exodus 1:22—2:9) or a children's Bible storybook, such as *Barnabas Children's Bible*, No. 42.
- Thomas Barnardo: in Victorian times he discovered children begging and sleeping rough and began a work that still continues, helping abused, neglected and vulnerable children (see www.barnardos.org.uk).
- C.T. Studd, the founder of WEC: with a vision to 'love God, and love your neighbour'. Find the story on the WEC website or in *Ten Boys Who Used Their Talents* by Irene Howat (Christian Focus Publications, 2008).
- WEC: an organisation that seeks to bring the gospel to unevangelised peoples and demonstrate the compassion of Christ in a needy world. Their vision is still that of their founder: 'Love God, and love your neighbour'. You can download free children's resources from their website, www.wec-int.org.uk.
- Focus on a local person, organisation or charity exhibiting and spreading God's love.

Find Jonathan's story in 1 Samuel 18:1–4; 19:1–10, 20; *Barnabas Children's Bible*, No. 122.

Find a hiding place, under a table or in a corner, to tell or read the story.

David made a hiding place in a field. I wonder why he did that…

David had been a shepherd but now he was winning lots of battles in King Saul's army. Jonathan was the king's son. Jonathan and David were best friends, but King Saul hated David. Twice King Saul tried to kill David with his spear. Jonathan told his father that David was his friend, and King Saul promised not to hurt David. But King Saul broke his promise and threw his spear angrily at David again.

David hid from King Saul in a field. Jonathan told King Saul that David was a good man and could be trusted, but King Saul even tried to kill Jonathan for being friends with David. Jonathan knew that David had to leave or be killed. Jonathan loved his father, the king, and he loved his best friend, David. Jonathan fired an arrow in the field where David was hiding, as a signal that David must run away. David and Jonathan made a promise always to be friends and always to care for each other.

Consider Jonathan's story

- What did we find out about David and Jonathan in that story?
- I wonder what makes a good best friend…
- The love and friendship that David and Jonathan had for each other came from God. All love comes from God and we can share it with each other.

Explore their story

Choose one or more activity, depending on your group and time.

1. Radio reporter

Imagine you are going to interview your chosen character. Help the children to work out some questions and answers. For example:

- Question: 'Jonathan, why did you try to persuade your father, the king, not to hurt David?'
- Answer: 'Because David was my best friend and I loved him. I wanted him to be safe, and for my father to accept him.'

Hold up your fist to your mouth as a microphone and ask the questions. Children can speak the answers into the microphone. Questions and answers can be written or pictures relating to the story can be drawn.

 Stick questions and answers or pictures in your story book.

2. Magazine reporter

Draw pictures or take photos of children posing the key parts of the story. Group-write a magazine article under a heading such as 'My best friend saved me!'

3. Playtime

Younger children can have a time of free play. If possible, include toys and puzzles that relate to families and friends, and encourage the children to show love to dolls, soft toys and each other.

♥ Respond

You may like to play a worship CD quietly in the background during this activity.

What about me?

Say: What do you think it means to be loving? Do you know that God wants us to be loving, like him? I would like to be loving, like God, and be like *[the character in your chosen story]*. Would you like to be loving and spread God's love around? I wonder what we could do that would be loving, that would spread God's love around…

Listen to the children's ideas, share your own and help them form some practical possibilities. Help each child write one idea on a red heart to take home.

Let's pray

Help children contribute specific ideas for prayer using the following pointers. Ask them if there is anything else they would like the group to pray for.

- Let's thank God that he's so loving.
- Sometimes we're not loving like God, and we can tell him that we're sorry.
- Sometimes it's hard to be loving like God, and we need to ask him to help us.

 Record particular prayer requests in your story book.

Review

Look back through your story book. Check where today's Bible stories fit in relation to others already in the book. Look at some previous prayer requests and find out if and how they have been answered. Note any answered prayers in the story book.

Way out

Eat the jam sandwiches that you made at the 'Way in' stage.

Say: Remember, God loves us. He wants us to spread his love everywhere we go. Not just when it's easy, with our families and friends, but when it's hard, with people we don't like or who are unkind to us.

Family follow-up

See www.barnabasinchurches.org.uk/extra-resources/ to download the family follow-up sheet.

Play

Stick a paper plate on to a lolly stick for each person. On one side draw a happy face and on the other side a sad face. Hold up the happy faces and, in turn, name a person who is easy to love. Hold up the sad faces and think of a person who is sometimes hard to love. Imagine sitting in the crowd on the hillside, listening to Jesus encourage us to love even those we don't want to love. How we need God's love to help us!

Add 'love' to your 'God is…' collage or patchwork.

Praise

Give each person a few words from the Bible verse to say in sequence. When the family is able to do that, fill a cup with water and slowly pour it into a bowl while the verse is being said. Can you get through the verse before the water runs out? Try again, pouring more slowly. We run out of our own love so quickly. We need more of God's love. We can praise him that he never, ever runs out of love and he will give us more when we ask him.

Write the verse, or random words from it, using magnetic letters, to remind everyone of the verse when they use the fridge. Younger children can spell out LOVE using magnetic fridge letters, alphabet bricks or letters shaped out of playdough.

The theme colour is red: making a strawberry jelly for tea or adding cherry tomatoes or red-coated small cheeses to lunchboxes can act as a reminder to behave in a loving way, as will looking out for the colour red as you are out and about—on flowers, berries, cars, postboxes and so on.

Plan

Explore one or more of the stories together.

When you're out and about, look out for people's loving actions, such as mothers shopping for the family's food, someone pushing a wheelchair, a teacher helping a child who has fallen, a child refusing to join in unkindness to someone and so on. Share these with the rest of the family.

Ask: 'What can we do as a family, or as individuals, to spread God's love to others, even to those who are unkind to us or upset us?' Draw small red hearts around the rim of your play activity paper plates, on the happy side, and write your ideas around the face. Keep the paper plates where they can be seen regularly as a reminder to check how everyone is doing.

Pray

Thank God for any specific ways in which he has shown his love to the family. Say sorry to God for particular times when we have not shown his love to others. Ask for God's help to spread his love in the ways we have identified.

❋

God is faithful

- **Theme:** We can keep faithful to God's word
- **Learn from Jesus:** Luke 4:16–21
- **Bible verse:** 'For the word of the Lord is right and true; he is faithful in all he does' (Psalm 33:4, NIV).
- **Discover other people's stories:** Ezra; Josiah; William Tyndale; Wycliffe Bible translators
- **Theme colour:** Orange

Way in

Spot the difference

Bring: Orange paper or cloth; cartons of orange juice and another orange coloured juice (mango, tropical and so on) with both cartons covered; oranges; cups

Cover a table with orange paper or cloth.

Say: I wonder why we are using the colour orange today…

Put everything on the table.

Say: I wonder what we could do with all these things…

Listen and affirm ideas without comment. Give everyone two cups and a taste of each juice.

Say: These cups of juice look the same. Do they taste the same? I wonder why they taste different…

Listen to children's answers and then uncover the cartons so everyone can see what they contain. Smell the oranges.

Say: Taste the juice again. Can you taste and smell which is the orange juice? Orange tastes and smells exactly like orange, because it is orange!

Learn from Jesus

Luke 4:16–21: Today's story is about God's promise to send someone very special to show and tell exactly what God is like. People wrote down carefully what God said about this person. Hundreds of years later, when Jesus came, he was exactly as God said he would be. Jesus grew up in a small town where everybody knew him. They knew his parents and his brothers and sisters. They thought Jesus was just an ordinary boy, but Jesus wasn't ordinary. Jesus is God's Son, the very special person that God had promised to send.

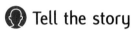 Tell the story

Choose the story option most appropriate for your group.

1. Waiting time

Practise whispering the phrase 'We're waiting, we're waiting', tapping the rhythm on table or knees.

Say: As I tell the story, watch for my arm going up, and then you can keep whispering these words until I put it down again.

Jesus had been here, there and everywhere, making people well, showing and telling everyone how much God loved them. He was God's good news! Then one day he came to his own town. He went to the synagogue where people went to learn about God and hear God's words. *(Raise your arm and encourage the whispering to begin.)*

Jesus walked to the front and took God's words in his hands. He read out loud God's promise to send a very special person who would make people well and show and tell exactly what God is like. Then he sat down and said, 'That's me. I'm the one.' *(Put your arm down.)*

People had been waiting and waiting and waiting for hundreds of years but, now that he was here, they didn't believe he was God's promise.

They said, 'But he's just someone from our town!'

'Who does he think he is?'

'He can't be the special person we've been waiting for!'

But they were wrong. Jesus was the one God had promised. Jesus did and said exactly what God had told people to write down, so long ago. Jesus was sad that people in his town didn't believe him. He went away, making people well in other places, showing and telling exactly what God is like.

2. Scrolls

If you have internet access, you can show the children some web pictures of Bible scrolls. Alternatively, you could save the pictures to a laptop or print them out in advance. Explain that, in Jesus' time, Old Testament scripture was written down on scrolls as God's word and read out to people in the synagogue.

Help children to find the opening verses of Isaiah 61 and compare them with Luke 4:18–19.

Say: Hundreds of years earlier, God had told Isaiah the prophet the good news that he would send someone to show and tell exactly what God is like. Isaiah wrote down God's words and Jesus read them out in the synagogue in his home town. Then Jesus told everyone that scripture had come true, right there in that place, in front of them. People were shocked. They didn't believe Jesus. To them, he was just a man from their village. Most of them had known him since he was a small boy. How could he possibly be God's special, chosen, holy one? Jesus went away without blessing the people there with miracles of healing, but, wherever else he went, there were some who believed he was exactly the one God had promised.

3. Find the story in the Bible

An adult or child, or everyone together, may read from a children's Bible storybook such as *Barnabas Children's Bible*, No. 259.

Consider the story

- I wonder how Jesus felt when the people in the synagogue didn't believe him…
- I wonder what we would have thought if we had been there…
- What did we find out about Jesus and God in that story?
- In what ways is Jesus faithful, just like God?

🖐 Explore the story

Choose one or more activity, depending on your group and time.

1. Just like me!

> **Bring:** A camera; paper; pencils

Put the group into pairs and ask everyone to draw a picture of their partner's face. Name the pictures and spread them out.

Say: Are these pictures an exact copy of the people we have drawn? I wonder how we could get an exact copy...

Take a photograph of everyone in turn.

Say: Now we have an exact copy. God didn't give a photograph of what Jesus would look like, but he did give details of what his special, chosen, holy one would do and be like. Jesus was exactly what God had promised in every detail.

NB: If you don't have parental permission to take photographs, make sure you delete the pictures before the end of the session.

📖 Stick your pictures, and possibly the photos you print off later, in your story book.

2. Hand in hand

> **Bring:** Thick orange paint; tray

Say: What's today's colour? We are using orange as the colour of God's faithfulness.

Squeeze or mix orange paint on to the tray. Press your hands into the paint and press them on to paper. Make another copy underneath without dipping your hands into the paint. Help the children to do the same.

Say: Are both handprints the same? One is clearer and better than the other, but Jesus is an exact copy of God's word. Jesus was faithful to God's word.

📖 When dry, cut out the handprints and stick them in your story book. Add Psalm 33:4.

♥ Time to praise God

Hold up a Bible. Explain that the Bible story told us that Jesus was faithful to God's word in every way. Jesus shows us what God is like. God is faithful.

It tells us in the Bible

For the word of the Lord is right and true; he is faithful in all he does. (Psalm 33:4)

Find and read the Bible verse. In pairs, one partner says the first part of the verse and makes up simple hand or feet actions, and the other partner responds with the second part, copying the actions exactly.

Music praise

You can sing together or along with a CD or DVD. Some children may prefer to do actions, dance or jump around rather than sing. Alternatively, you can play a CD while doing the 'scrolls' activity. Choose songs relating to God's faithfulness (see page 19 for suggested CDs). Younger children might like to try the following action song to the tune 'London's burning'.

God is faithful, God is faithful! (Clap hands above heads.)
Sending Jesus, sending Jesus! (Wave goodbye with both hands.)
Jesus! Jesus! (Hold out hands in welcome.)
We can praise him, we can praise him! (Wave hands in the air.)

Activity options

1. Scrolls

Bring: Frieze paper; ribbon; 15cm x 1cm dowelling sticks (optional)

Use an internet translator such as Google Language Tools to translate Psalm 33:4 into Hebrew, and print it out. Children can try to copy it on to a strip of paper, writing the verse in English underneath. Alternatively, just write the verse in English. Show how to roll up the scrolls from each end into the centre and tie with ribbon. If you wish, you can use dowelling sticks to make the scrolls stronger.

2. Simon says

Play a game of 'Simon says' or 'Follow my leader' with actions for everyone to copy.

Discover other people's stories

Choose from the options below to discover people who were (or are) inspired to be faithful, like God.

Tell their story and discuss how they show God's faithfulness through their actions.

- Ezra: he read God's law to the people. Find the story below.
- Josiah: he rediscovered the scrolls containing God's law and had them read to the people. Find the story in your Bible: 2 Kings 22—23 or a children's Bible story book such as *Barnabas Children's Bible*, No. 203.
- William Tyndale: against the wishes of the church, he translated the Bible into English so that everyone could read it for themselves. Find the story on www.tyndale.org; in *William Tyndale* (Torchlighters DVD) or in *Ten Boys Who Made a Difference* by Irene Howat (Christian Focus Publications, 2010).
- Wycliffe Bible Translators: an organisation dedicated to translating the Bible into every language. Search for the story of Cameron Townsend, and download free children's resources from the website www.wycliffe.org.uk. Find resources for older children on www.wynetuk.org.
- Focus on someone in your church with a story to tell about being faithful to God's word.

Find Ezra's story in Nehemiah 8—9; *Barnabas Children's Bible*, No. 238.

Bring: Construction bricks; pictures of walled cities (optional)

Using construction bricks, help children to build a square wall as high as possible, with gaps for gates. Show any pictures you have and talk about why people built walled cities in times past and what happened when enemies came to fight. While building, begin to tell the story expressively, breaking in where necessary to give instructions for the wall.

Long ago, God's people lost a battle and were taken far, far away by their enemies. Everything that was precious was taken away, too, even God's laws from the temple, but everything was kept safe in the new country. Many years later, the king allowed some of God's people go back to their own country. The king gave God's laws back to Ezra the priest and he took them carefully back to Jerusalem.

The great wall around Jerusalem was completely broken down. It had to be built all over again so that people could live safely inside the city. Nehemiah organised the wall-building, and every family had a piece of wall to build.

When it was finished, a high platform was built for Ezra the priest, and all the people came to listen to him. He unrolled God's word and began to read out loud God's laws. The people all stood up because God's laws are holy. As they heard God's laws, they praised God and worshipped him, kneeling with their faces on the ground. Then they became sad because they had not known or kept God's laws. Ezra told them not to be sad. It was a good day because now they knew God's laws. Everyone joined in a feast to celebrate.

After the feast, the people came back to Ezra and told God how sorry they were for not keeping his laws. They said sorry for their parents and grandparents, because they hadn't lived right, either. They were so glad to hear and know God's laws and to be able to live his way.

Consider Ezra's story

- What did we find out about Ezra in that story?
- I wonder how Ezra felt when at last he could stand up and read out God's laws…
- Ezra brought the people back to God.
- Ezra was faithful to God's word.

Explore their story

Choose one or more activity, depending on your group and time.

1. Fedele!

Use an internet translator such as Google Language Tools to translate 'God is faithful' into as many different languages as possible. Shout them out one by one and let the children shout them back to you.

Stick your 'God is faithful' list in your story book.

2. Tap and rap

Explain that you are going to tap out a tune on the table and, when the children recognise it, they can join in. Choose a simple and easily recognisable tune. Some children might like to try to choose and tap their own choice for everyone to copy.

3. Playtime

Younger children can have a time of free play. If possible, include toys and puzzles that reflect the idea of a faithful representation—for example, sorting bricks or socks into colours or pairs, or simple jigsaws with a picture to copy.

Respond

You may like to play a worship CD quietly in the background during this activity.

What about me?

Bring: Orange-scented candle; matches; orange paper

Put the candle in a safe, supervised place and light it.

Say: What do you think it means to be faithful to God's word? Do you know that God wants us to be faithful, like him? I would like to be faithful to God's word and be like *[the character in your chosen story]*. Would you like to be faithful to God's word? I wonder how we could be faithful to God's word…

Listen to the children's ideas, share your own and help them form some practical possibilities. Help each child draw an orange-sized circle on orange paper, cut it out and write one idea on it to take home.

Let's pray

Help the children to contribute ideas for prayer, using the following pointers. Ask them if there is anything else they would like the group to pray for.

- Let's thank God that he is so faithful.
- Sometimes we don't want to know what God says, or we forget or disobey it, and we can tell God that we're sorry.
- Sometimes it's hard to keep faithful to God's word, especially when others don't. We can ask him to help us.

 Record particular prayer requests in your story book.

Review

Look back through your story book. Check where today's Bible stories fit in relation to others already in the book. Look at some previous prayer requests and find out if and how they have been answered. Note any answered prayers in the story book.

Way out

Give everyone an orange from your 'Way in' activity, as a reminder of their plans to keep faithful to God's word.

Say: Remember, God is faithful in sending Jesus, and Jesus was faithful to God's word.

Family follow-up

See www.barnabasinchurches.org.uk/extra-resources/ to download the family follow-up sheet.

Play

Make a wordsearch including the word 'faithful' as many times as possible—forwards, backwards, up, down, diagonal and so on. Use orange highlighters to find the words. For younger children, make some simple dot-to-dot pictures to be joined up with orange pens.

Add 'faithful' to your 'God is...' collage or patchwork.

Praise

Make up a simple tune to sing the words of the Bible verse. If anyone plays a musical instrument, they could practise an accompaniment, or use pots and pans as drums and containers of rice or pasta as shakers. When you eat together, sing the verse at the end of the meal. Hide magnetic letters of the word 'faithful' around the house for children to find and then place them on the fridge as a reminder for everyone.

The theme colour is orange: having orange juice or marmalade at breakfast time, or adding satsumas or small cartons of orange juice to lunch boxes, can act as a reminder to be faithful to God's word, as can looking out for the colour orange as you are out and about (on vegetables, flowers, animals, fish and so on).

Plan

Explore one or more of the stories together.

When you're out and about, if opportunities arise, talk about people who break the law by making fake designer gear, trainers, watches, DVDs and so on. Explain that these are not faithful copies.

Ask: How can we as a family, or as individuals, be faithful to God's word? Set a bowl of oranges on a table. Write out your ideas with an orange felt pen and tuck them into the bowl. Each time an orange is eaten, check on the ideas to see how they are working out.

Pray

Thank God for any specific ways in which he has shown his faithfulness to the family. Say sorry to God for particular times when we have not been faithful to God's word. Ask for God's help to follow through the ideas for being faithful to his word.

✳

God is patient

> - Theme: Learning to be patient, like Jesus
> - Learn from Jesus: Mark 14:26–42
> - Bible verse: 'The Lord isn't slow about keeping his promises, as some people think he is. In fact, God is patient' (2 Peter 3:9a).
> - Discover other people's stories: Ezra; Jacob; Joni Eareckson Tada; Gladys Aylward
> - Theme colour: Yellow

Way in

Cake!

> Bring: Yellow paper or cloth; a cake sandwiched with lemon curd and topped with yellow icing, or biscuits with yellow icing, in a tin

Cover a table with yellow paper or cloth.

Say: I wonder why we are using the colour yellow today...

Put the cake tin on the table.

Say: I wonder what's in this tin...

Listen and affirm ideas without comment. Open the tin to show the cake.

Say: I wonder what we could do with this cake...

Listen to ideas, and then *Say:* I'm sorry, but it's not time to eat the cake yet. We shall just have to be patient and wait until later.

Learn from Jesus

Mark 14:26–42: Today's story is about when Jesus was getting ready to leave his friends. It was nearly time for Jesus to go back to God in heaven. It was part of God's plan for Jesus to die, and soon soldiers would come to take him away.

Jesus and his friends had just eaten their last meal together and he wanted to keep his friends very close for this last little time.

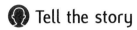 Tell the story

Choose the story option most appropriate for your group.

The butterfly watched the four men come into the garden. It was very late and dark, but the moon was bright and full, shining through the trees. Three of the men sat down against a tree. The butterfly heard them call the one who walked away 'Jesus'. Jesus stopped close to the butterfly. The butterfly could see that his face was sweating, even though it was a cold night. Jesus walked up and down, very bothered. Jesus was talking to his dad. He said, 'Is there any other way to do this… please? But if you really want me to, I will.' He looked very sad and lonely.

Jesus went over to his friends and the butterfly saw that they were all asleep. Jesus spoke to one of them, asking him to stay awake and pray for him. Jesus came back, walking up and down, and cried out the same things to his dad, so very upset. Again, he went over to the others, who were asleep again and snoring. Jesus came away again, walking up and down and asking his dad for help.

Then the butterfly saw Jesus wake his sleeping friends. He said, 'Wake up. Here is our friend, bringing the soldiers to take me away.' The butterfly knew that Jesus was in big trouble and wondered where Jesus' dad was. Jesus' dad was God in heaven, and he was helping Jesus to stick to the big plan.

1. Butterfly puppet

To make a butterfly puppet, draw five teardrop shapes on paper, about the length of your middle finger, and cut them out: one for the body and four for the wings. Pattern the wings with yellow felt-tipped pens and stick them on to the body. Make feelers by cutting out two thin strips of paper, curling the ends round a pen and sticking them to the back of the head. Finally, cut a strip of paper to fit around your index finger and fix the butterfly to it.

Use the finger puppet to help tell the story.

2. Troubled tracks

Ask everyone to draw a tree and three simple figures lying against it. Tell the story without reference to the butterfly. Using thick yellow felt-tipped pens, draw arrows to track Jesus walking up and down, backwards and forwards, on his own.

3. Find the story in the Bible

An adult or child may read Mark 14:26–42 from a Bible or children's Bible storybook such as *Barnabas Children's Bible*, No. 304.

Consider the story

- Jesus really needed his friends just then. I wonder why he let them sleep so long…
- I wonder what we would have thought if we had been one of them…
- What did we find out about Jesus in that story?
- In what ways is Jesus patient, just like God?

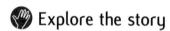 Explore the story

Choose one or more of the activities, depending on your group and time.

1. Waiting

Bring: A year planner; yellow highlighter pen

Everyone can mark their birthdays on the calendar with the highlighter pen. Discuss how hard it can be to wait for birthdays, and the need for patience. Refer to the yellow cake still waiting to be eaten.

Say: We need to be patient just a little longer and then it will be the right time to eat it.

 Stick the calendar in your story book.

2. Snakes alive!

> **Bring:** Snakes and ladders game

Play a game of snakes and ladders.

Say: Just when we think we are getting near the top, we can find ourselves down near the bottom again. It's not always easy to be patient.

3. Caterpillar crawl

> **Bring:** Yellow playdough; a book showing the life cycle of a butterfly or *The Very Hungry Caterpillar* by Eric Carle (Puffin, 2011)

Use the playdough to make caterpillars. Try to fix them to a window or wall. Show and tell how the caterpillar becomes a chrysalis and then a butterfly.

Say: The caterpillar can't hurry or skip a stage. It has to eat and wait and be patient. We're waiting patiently for that cake, too!

If you have time, everyone can make butterfly finger puppets as above.

♥ Time to praise God

Hold up a Bible. Explain that the Bible story told us that Jesus was patient with his friends, even though they let him down so badly and couldn't keep awake to wait with him and pray. Jesus is patient. Jesus shows us what God is like. God is patient.

It tells us in the Bible

The Lord isn't slow about keeping his promises, as some people think he is. In fact, God is patient. (2 Peter 3:9a)

> **Bring:** Thin card; a large plate; a split-pin fastener

Draw round a large plate and cut out the circle. Divide the rim into 20 spaces, one for each word of the verse plus the whole reference. Together, fill in the words. Draw, colour yellow and cut out clock hands. Fix them in the centre of the circle with a split-pin fastener. Take turns to move the hands while you repeat the verse.

Say: When we have to wait for something, time seems to move very slowly. God is patient and keeps his promises to us at just the right time.

 Stick the clock in your story book.

Music praise

You can sing together or sing along with a CD or DVD. Some children may prefer to do actions, dance or jump around rather than sing. Alternatively, you can play a CD while doing the Bible verse activity. Choose songs relating to God's patience (see page 19 for suggested CDs).

Activity options

1. Stamp it out!

Repeat the rhyme below three times, first with a loud voice and stamping, then with a normal voice and clapping, and finally with whispering and tapping.

God is patient. God is great!
God is patient, never, never late!
We find it hard to wait and wait,
But God is patient. God is great!

2. Patient praise!

> **Bring:** Thick yellow paint; kitchen roll

Pour yellow paint on to your hands, rub them together, blot on kitchen roll and wave to dry.
    Sing the praise song below to the tune 'Here we go round the mulberry bush'.

God's not slow to keep his word. (Clap own hands, clap partner's. Repeat.)
Keep his word, keep his word. (Clap own hands, clap partner's. Repeat.)
God's not slow to keep his word. (Clap own hands, clap partner's. Repeat.)
He is always patient. (Face partner and wave hands in the air)

Wash hands or keep them yellow as a reminder that God is patient.

At the beginning of the activity, make a set of yellow prints to put in the story book. Add the Bible verse.

Discover other people's stories

Choose from the options below to discover people who learnt to be patient, like God.

Tell their story and discuss how they showed God's patience through their actions.

- Exiles in Babylon: they waited patiently for God to keep his promise of a return to Jerusalem. Find the story below.
- Jacob: worked for Laban for 14 years so that he could marry Rachel. Find the story in your Bible: Genesis 29:1–30 or a children's Bible storybook such as *Barnabas Children's Bible*, No. 25.
- Joni Eareckson Tada: paralysed in a diving accident, Joni's very human story exudes patience and trust in God and can be found in *Ten Girls Who Changed the World*, Irene Howat (Christian Focus 4Kids, 2008).
- Gladys Aylward: sure of her call to China, Gladys learned to be patient and await God's timing. Find her story on Torchlighters *Heroes of the Faith* DVD.
- Focus on a local person, organisation or charity exhibiting patience.

Find the exiles' story in Ezra 1—2; *Barnabas Children's Bible*, No. 225

Bring: Gold and silver chocolate coins; cloth bag

Sit around a table and demonstrate actions for the children to copy as the story progresses.

Long ago, God's people had lost a battle and been taken far, far away by their enemies. All the precious things from the temple in Jerusalem were taken away, too, but they were kept safe in the new country. God promised that one day his people would go back to Jerusalem and their own country.

God's people waited and waited for many years. (*Everyone lean on the table, head in hands, and sigh.*)

And then they waited more long years. (*Everyone lean on the table, head in hands, and sigh.*)

God's people knew that one day God would keep his promise. (*Everyone lean on the table, head in hands, and sigh.*)

They just had to be patient, and wait. (*Everyone lean on the table, head in hands, and sigh.*)

At long last, God told the king it was time to let some of his people go back to Jerusalem and build the temple that had been broken down in the battle. At long last, God's people would be able to worship God in the temple again. The king allowed God's people to collect gold and silver to take with them, and they could take back all the precious things that had been kept safe. (*Tip the chocolate coins into the bag. Let everyone shake the bag.*)

Not everyone went back straight away. Some had to be patient for a while longer and then the king would let them go, too. Everyone was so happy. At long last, God had kept his promise.

Consider the exiles' story

- What did we find out about God's people in that story?
- I wonder how the people felt when, at long last, God told the king they could go back to Jerusalem…
- God's people were patient through long years of waiting.
- All patience comes from God.

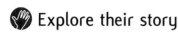 Explore their story

Choose one or more activity, depending on your group and time.

1. At last!

Bring: A camera

Talk about how long your chosen character(s) had to be patient: for some, it was (or is) a lifetime. How would their lives be impacted? What might have been different? Compile a list.

Say: We've been patient for only a little while but now we can eat our cake.

Share out the cake. Take a photograph of the cake and those enjoying it, or draw pictures of the cake.

Put photographs or drawings of the cake in the story book, together with the list.

2. Grandmother's keys

Bring: A bunch of keys; a blindfold

Choose someone who is happy to be blindfolded to sit crosslegged a distance away, with their back to the others. Place the keys in front of them.

Say: The rest of us are going to creep very slowly towards [name the sitting person], as quietly as possible. If [name] hears a noise, she/he will point towards the noise. If you are pointed at, you can sit down. If someone gets really close, they must be patient, and very slowly and carefully try to pick up the keys without [name] hearing them. If they are heard, they can sit down.

Depending on time, play the game several times.

3. Playtime

If possible, include toys and puzzles that reflect the idea of time and patience, such as old clocks and watches or a magnetic fishing game.

♥ Respond

You may like to play a worship CD quietly in the background during the activity below.

What about me?

> Bring: Yellow sticky notes

Say: What do you think it means to be patient? Do you know that God wants us to be patient, like him? I would like to be patient like God, and be like *[the character in your chosen story]*. Would you like to be patient, like God? I wonder what we could do that would help us to be more patient…

Listen to the children's ideas, share your own and help them form some practical possibilities. Help each child write one idea on a yellow sticky note to take home.

Let's pray

Help children contribute specific ideas for prayer, using the following pointers. Ask them if there is anything else they would like the group to pray for.

- Let's thank God that he's so patient.
- Sometimes we're not patient like God, and we can tell him that we're sorry.
- Sometimes it's hard to be patient like God, and we need to ask him to help us.

 Record particular prayer requests in your story book.

Review

Look back through your story book. Check where today's Bible stories fit in relation to others already in the book. Look at some previous prayer requests and find out if and how they have been answered. Note any answered prayers in the story book.

Way out

Give a yellow felt-tipped pen to each child.

Say: Every time you use a yellow pen to colour something, you can remember that God is patient and he wants us to be patient, too.

Family follow-up

See www.barnabasinchurches.org.uk/extra-resources/ to download the family follow-up sheet.

Play

Butterfly painting

Fold a sheet of paper in half and paint a simple butterfly body and head, centre left of the crease. Paint in one feeler, top left. Paint two yellow wings, attached to the body on the left-hand side of the paper. Carefully fold the paper in half and press down firmly. Open out the paper and allow the paint to dry. When dry, the butterfly can be cut out and placed in a prominent position as a reminder of God's patience.

Show children how to play Patience or Solitaire on the computer or with a pack of cards.

Make real custard together instead of instant custard. Most of us want things done quickly and easily, but patience can produce something much better.

Add 'patient' to 'God is…' on your collage or patchwork.

Praise

Explore online images from the Book of Kells, a book of the four Gospels patiently produced and beautifully illustrated by monks around AD800. Write and decorate the Bible verse in this style.

The theme colour is yellow. Keeping a daily count of yellow cars, having a weather chart showing how much sun is seen each day or planning a day when everyone wears as much yellow as possible are all ways to remind everyone to be more patient.

Plan

Explore one or more of the stories together.

When you're out and about, be aware of opportunities for patience, such as taking turns, waiting for a free petrol pump, queuing in the supermarket, challenging children, hurrying a conversation and so on. Share attitudes and responses with the family.

Ask: What can we do as a family, or as individuals, to become more patient and to encourage each other? If you have made the paper butterflies, ideas can be written across the wings. Alternatively, use yellow sticky notes and write ideas on them, sticking them on the fridge.

Pray

Thank God for any specific ways in which he has shown patience with the family. Say sorry to God for particular times when we have not been patient. Ask for God's help to become more patient.

✳

God is powerful

- **Theme**: Discovering God's power at work in us
- **Learn from Jesus**: Mark 4:35–41
- **Bible verse**: 'You alone work miracles, and you have let nations see your mighty power' (Psalm 77:14).
- **Discover other people's stories**: Joseph; Brother Andrew; Smith Wigglesworth
- **Theme colour**: Purple

Way in

Puff and blow!

Bring: Purple paper or cloth; purple balloons; a hand-operated balloon pump; purple parcel ribbon; scissors

Cover a table with purple paper or cloth.

Say: I wonder why we are using the colour purple today…

Put the items on the table.

Say: I wonder what we could do with these things…

Listen and affirm ideas without comment. Talk briefly about the power of air or wind, seen in windmills, sail boats, wind instruments, kites, wind turbines generating electricity and so on.

Inflate enough balloons for your chosen activities, cut lengths of parcel ribbon and tie to the neck of the balloons. Keep uninflated balloons for everyone for the 'Respond' activity.

Learn from Jesus

Mark 4:35–41: Today's story is about Jesus showing God's amazing power. Wherever Jesus went, people followed. One day, Jesus had been talking to crowds by the lake for hours and by the evening he was very tired. If Jesus went to a friend's house, people would follow. Then Jesus had a great idea. Some of his friends were fishermen, with a boat. If they crossed the lake in the boat, then people wouldn't be able to follow. Best of all, Jesus could have a sleep in the boat. So that's what they did, but on the way something amazing happened.

🔊 Tell the story

Choose the story option most appropriate for your group.

Jesus and his friends pushed the boat off the beach and climbed aboard. Jesus lay down, and soon the gentle waves rocked him to sleep. The wind filled the sail and the boat headed for the other side of the lake. But then the wind blew stronger and stronger and the waves grew higher and higher. The water came over the sides of the boat. In the darkness, everyone else, cold and wet and very scared, held on tightly to the mast to stop themselves being swept into the water, but Jesus was still fast asleep. His friends shook him awake, asking him to save them.

Jesus stood up and looked at the stormy waves and heard the howling wind. Jesus told the wind to stop. Jesus told the waves to lie down quietly— and they did! Just like that. Not gradually, but dead stop. Jesus asked his friends why they were afraid. Didn't they know that with Jesus they were safe?

His friends could hardly believe what they had seen. So much power! Jesus! They knew that that kind of power was God's power.

1. Sail away!

> **Bring:** Broom handle; purple fabric

Tie the fabric to the broom handle to make a mast and sail. Sit on the floor, as if you are in a boat, with someone holding the mast and sail. Add actions as you tell the story.

2. Stormy sounds

Tell the story. Have everyone suggest simple sound effects for the growing storm and howling winds, using mouths, hands and feet, leading to the sudden silence when Jesus spoke to the wind and waves. Read the story again with accompanying sounds.

3. Find the story in the Bible

An adult or child may read Mark 4:35–41 from a Bible or children's Bible storybook such as *Barnabas Children's Bible*, No. 270.

Consider the story

- I wonder how Jesus managed to sleep through the storm…
- I wonder why the wind and waves obeyed Jesus….
- What did we find out about Jesus in that story?
- In what ways is Jesus is powerful, like God?

Explore the story

Choose one or more activity, depending on your group and time.

1. Blow hard!

Bring: Purple feathers (available from craft shops), or balloons

Throw a feather up in the air and try to keep it aloft by blowing. No hands! Who has the power to keep a feather in the air for the longest time? Have someone count as each person tries, to find the winner.

Say: We haven't got the power even to stop a feather from falling down for long. Jesus has the power to stop the wind and waves of a storm.

 Stick a feather or deflated balloon in your story book.

2. Straight to the line!

> **Bring:** Drinking straws

Mark out a start and finish line. The aim is to use the drinking straw to try to blow a balloon, in as straight a line as possible, to the finish.

Say: We can't even control wind power through a drinking straw. Jesus has power over the wind and waves.

3. Wind power

Form a circle. Say the rhyme aloud with an expressive voice and actions for children to copy.

The wind wafts softly through the trees.
It's nothing more than a gentle breeze.
But stronger and stronger it blows around,
Till the branches almost touch the ground.
Can't see the wind, but I hear it howl.
Now it sounds more like a growl.
Louder, louder, and with a 'crack!'
The tallest tree falls on its back.

Say: However powerful the wind, God's power is greater.

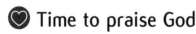 Time to praise God

Hold up a Bible. Explain that the Bible story told us that Jesus has power over the wind and the waves. Jesus shows us what God is like. God is powerful.

It tells us in the Bible

You alone work miracles, and you have let nations see your mighty power. (Psalm 77:14)

> **Bring:** Purple fabric; purple felt-tipped pen; small pieces of paper

Using a purple pen, write out each word of the verse and reference on separate small pieces of paper. Place them in the centre of the purple fabric and gather it up.

Everyone stands in a large circle around you. Release the papers from the material, high into the air. Have everyone find the words and place them in order on the material, finally reading them aloud together.

 Stick the words in order in your story book.

Music praise

You can sing together or along with a CD or DVD. Some children may prefer to do actions, dance or jump around rather than sing. Alternatively, you can play a CD while doing the Bible verse activity. Choose songs relating to God's power (see page 19 for suggested CDs).

Activity options

1. Praise practice

Listen to the song 'What noise shall we make?' Go through the verses so that children can experiment and decide on their individual noises. Sing the song together.

Say: We are praising our powerful God.

2. Purple praise

Bring: String; purple drinking straws, cut into 1cm lengths; cellophane squares, foil cake cases, sweet wrappers or similar; hole punch

Cut a length of string for each person and wrap a piece of sticky tape around one end so that it can be used to thread. Punch holes in the centre of cellophane squares, cake cases or sweet wrappers. Thread these materials on to the strings, then join them all together to make a garland.

Everyone can take turns to swing the garland through the air, wriggle it along the floor, make waves and so on, while others jump over and run underneath.

Say: We can praise Jesus because he has power over the wind and waves.

Discover other people's stories

Choose from the options below to discover people who depended on God's power.

Tell their story and discuss how they show God's power through their actions.

- David: a young man who was determined that God should be known as the greatest. Find the story below.
- Joseph: through good times and bad, God's power shone through his life. Find the story in your Bible: Genesis 41:47—45:28 or a children's Bible storybook such as *Barnabas Children's Bible*, Nos. 34–39.
- Brother Andrew: a man who depended on God's power in dangerous circumstances, serving persecuted Christians across the world. Find his story in *God's Smuggler* by John and Elizabeth Sherrill (Hodder & Stoughton, 2008) or in *Ten Boys Who Changed the World* by Irene Howat. See also www.opendoorsuk.org for Kidzone resources.
- Smith Wigglesworth: an ordinary person who was filled with God's extraordinary power to heal. Find his story in *A Life Ablaze with the Power of God* by William Hacking (Harrison House, 2009).
- Focus on a local person with a testimony to God's power in their life.

Find David's story in 1 Samuel 17:1–50; *Barnabas Children's Bible*, No. 120.

Bring: Toy soldiers or play figures

Use the toy soldiers to show how battles were sometimes fought in Bible times, with the two sides lined up opposite each other. The strongest, biggest and fittest person from each side was chosen. These two champions fought each other in the centre, cheered on by their own side. The one who was left alive at the end of the fight won the victory for his side and their enemies had to accept it.

The battle lines were drawn between the Israelites and the Philistines. The Philistines put forward a huge giant of a man called Goliath to fight for them. The Israelites were all terrified of him and no Israelite would stand forward to fight him. Day after day, Goliath tramped up and down to shout that the Israelites were all cowards and weaklings.

One day, David came to the Israelite camp, bringing food for the army because his brothers were in the battle lines. David was too young and too small to fight and he watched Goliath strut up and down, shouting as usual. David was very angry. The Israelites were God's people. God's people! Surely God was on their side and would give them power to fight an unbeliever like Goliath? But no one would listen to David, and his brothers were embarrassed to hear him saying such things.

King Saul heard about David's anger and sent for him. The king said that David was far too young and too small to fight Goliath, but David insisted that God would give him the power to do the job. So King Saul had David dressed in his own armour. It didn't fit, of course, so David went out to meet Goliath without any armour. David only took with him the sling that he used to fight wild beasts and stop them coming near the animals he looked after.

David calmly looked for some smooth pebbles to put in his sling. Young David shouted to Goliath that he came in the name of the Lord Almighty, the God of the armies of Israel, and that Goliath would die because God's power is greater than any other. David put one stone in his sling and sent it whizzing across the space at Goliath. The stone hit Goliath in the head and killed him.

When the Philistines saw what David, with God's power, had done, they turned and ran.

Consider David's story

- What did we find out about David in that story?
- I wonder how David felt when there was no one on his side brave enough to face Goliath…

- David really needed God's power to help him beat Goliath, and God gave it to him.
- God gives his power to those who need it.

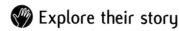 Explore their story

Choose one or more of the activities, depending on your group and time.

1. Cartoon capers

> **Bring:** A comic Bible or newspaper cartoon strip as an example; sheets of A4 paper; purple felt-tipped pens

Divide sheets of paper into eight boxes. Decide on eight scenes that tell your chosen story. Using purple felt-tipped pens, everyone can draw their own comic strip.

 Stick cartoon strips in the story book.

2. Playtime

Younger children can have a time of free play. If possible, include toys and puzzles that reflect the idea of power, such as blowing bubbles, pull-back-and-go cars, magnets and so on.

♥ Respond

You may like to play a worship CD quietly in the background during this activity.

What about me?

> **Bring:** String; labels

Say: What do you think it means to be powerful? Do you know that God can give us his power? I would like to have God's power in my life and be like *[the character in your chosen story]*. Would you like to have God's power in your life? I wonder what we might need God's power for…

Listen to the children's ideas, share your own and help them form some practical possibilities, writing them on small pieces of paper. Help everyone fold their paper and put it inside a balloon. Inflate the balloons, tie them off, and add the string with a named label.

Let's pray

Help children to contribute specific ideas for prayer, using the following pointers. Ask if there is anything else they would like the group to pray for.

- Let's thank God for his great power.
- We can tell God what we need.
- We can ask God for his power to help to change things.

🔖 If you would like to do so, record particular prayer requests in your story book.

Review

Look back through your story book. Check where today's Bible stories fit in relation to others already in the book. Look at some previous prayer requests and find out if and how they have been answered. Note any answered prayers in the story book.

Way out

Make sure everyone has their named balloon to take home as a reminder of God's power to help.

Say: Remember, God is powerful! God is great!

Family follow-up

See www.barnabasinchurches.org.uk/extra-resources/ to download the family follow-up sheet.

Play

Try this experiment to show the pushing power of air. Put a large plastic freezer bag, without holes, flat on a table with the top third (the open end) hanging over the edge. Place a large book on the rest of the bag on the table and have someone sit on it. Make a mouthpiece with the open end of the bag and blow into it. Keep blowing hard. What a surprise!

Experience God's power on a windy day with a Frisbee or kite, or experiment with making parachutes, using carrier bags, string and matchboxes. Use the internet to find photos of wind turbines: visit www.yes2wind.com to find out more about them. Are there any turbines in your area to go and look at?

Remembering Jesus' power over the wind and waves, use bath time or a paddling pool to test items that can sink or float. What happens if you put a small lump of playdough in the water? What happens if you flatten out the playdough? Make paper boats to float on large waves.

Add 'powerful' to your 'God is…' collage or patchwork.

Praise

Each day, draw on purple paper and cut out a few letters of the words of the Bible verse. When all the letters have been cut out, everyone can help put the words together in the right order and fix them to a door with sticky tack. Purple is the colour of kingly power. God is the great king and has all power.

The theme colour is purple. Eating some purple fruits or vegetables, such as black grapes, plums, purple sprouting broccoli or aubergines, or crushing some lavender into paper bags and placing them inside a pillowcase, can act as reminders of God's power.

Plan

Explore one or more of the stories together.

When you're out and about, see and appreciate God's power in creating stars and galaxies. Plan a visit to a planetarium or a late-night trip to an open space to look at the night sky.

Ask: How can God's power be shown in our life together as a family or as individuals? Fix family photos in and around the Bible verse on the door and keep in mind God's power to help change circumstances.

Pray

Thank God for any particular ways in which he has given his power to help change situations. Say sorry if there have been times when we have forgotten to ask for his power to help. Ask God for opportunities to show his power in our lives.

✳

God is good

- **Theme:** Showing God's goodness to those who are unwell
- **Learn from Jesus:** Luke 17:11–19
- **Bible verse:** 'You are good to everyone, and you take care of all your creation' (Psalm 145:9).
- **Discover other people's stories:** Peter and John; Naaman's servant; Paul Brant; Leprosy Mission; Mercy Ships
- **Theme colour:** Blue

Way in

Bells

Bring: Blue paper or cloth; small handbell; box of blue plasters

Cover a table with blue paper or cloth.
    Say: I wonder why we are using the colour blue today…
    Put the bell on the table.
    Say: I wonder what this bell is for…
    Listen and affirm ideas without comment. Let everyone have a turn with the bell. Talk briefly about where we find bells and how they are used—for example, schools, church buildings, buses, hospitals, fire alarms, animal collars.

Learn from Jesus

Luke 17:11–19: Today's story tells of a time when Jesus showed God's goodness. In biblical times, people became ill just as we do, but they didn't have doctors or medicines like ours to help make them better. Leprosy is an infectious disease that can easily be cured now, but then it was a dreadful illness. If you caught it, you were sent away from your home and work and family and friends. You had to live with others who had leprosy, beg for food and ring a bell to warn people you were nearby.

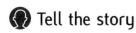 Tell the story

Choose the story option most appropriate for your group.

(Ring the bell once.) Jesus was on his way to Jerusalem with his friends. *(Ring the bell once.)* Just outside a village, Jesus heard some people calling to him, 'Jesus, Master, have pity on us!' *(Ring the bell once.)* Somehow, these men had heard about Jesus and the good things he did for people. They believed he could make them well again.

Jesus stopped and saw ten men with leprosy, ragged and sad. Jesus said, 'Go and show yourselves to the priests.' If anyone with leprosy believed they were better, they had to show the priest that the disease had gone. If he saw that it was true, they were allowed back home. *(Ring the bell once.)* The ten men went away quickly to find the priests. As they went, their leprosy was healed—completely gone. *(Ring the bell once.)*

Just one man came back and knelt at Jesus' feet to thank him, praising God for his goodness. *(Ring the bell once.)* Jesus asked him where the others were, and why they hadn't come back to praise God for his goodness. Then Jesus told him to get up and go home. His faith in Jesus had made him well again. He didn't need his bell any more.

1. Ding dong bell

Tell the story. At each ringing of the bell in the story, say, 'Ding-a-ling-ling'. Everyone repeats, with one person ringing the hand bell. Pass the bell on to someone else for the next occurrence.

2. Sounds of life

Tell the story, stopping at each ringing of the bell to think about the following questions. Make up and write down an appropriate sound for each (be creative with voice, instruments and so on).

- How would it feel to have leprosy and leave home, family, friends and work? (Devastating, miserable…)
- How would it feel to beg for food and see people turn away from you? (Angry, sad…)
- How do you think they felt when they called out to Jesus? (Not sure; anxious…)
- How do you think they felt when Jesus said that? (Hopeful, worried….)
- How do you think they felt when they realised they were healed? (Amazed, full of joy…)
- What might the man have called out in praise to God? (Example: You are great and good, mighty God!)

Retell the story just using the sounds, finishing with praise to the goodness of God.

3. Find the story in the Bible

An adult or child may read Luke 17:11–19 from a Bible or children's Bible storybook such as *Barnabas Children's Bible*, No. 284.

Consider the story

- I wonder why the other nine men didn't come back to thank Jesus or praise God…
- I wonder what happened when they all arrived home…
- What did we find out about Jesus in that story?
- In what ways is Jesus good, just like God?

Explore the story

Choose one or more of the activities, depending your group and time.

1. Ten to one

Bring: Blue paper

Show how to make ten concertina people (ten linked people that fold down to one person). The children can give each one a different face. Sing and dance with the concertina people to the tune 'One man went to mow':

Ten men came along, came along to Jesus.
Ten men, nine men, eight men, seven men, six men, five men, four men, three men,
two men, one man in a group,
Came along to Jesus.

Jesus made them well, Jesus, only Jesus!
Ten men, nine men, eight men, seven men, six men, five men, four men, three men,
two men, one man in a group.
Jesus, only Jesus!

 Stick a set of concertina men in your story book.

2. Kim's game

> **Bring:** A tray; small medical items, such as a pack of blue sticking plasters, empty tablet box, empty medicine bottle, bandage, thermometer, antiseptic cream, throat lozenges, tweezers and so on; blue paper or blue cloth

Place everything on the tray and cover with the blue paper or blue cloth. Remove the cloth and show the items, explaining what everything is.

Say: These are all things we might use when we are unwell or hurt.

Cover the tray again and, while children close their eyes, remove one item. Give everyone a turn to say what is missing.

3. Goodness!

> **Bring:** Paint thickened with flour in two shades of blue; paintbrushes; strips cut from old cards with small v-shapes cut along one short edge of each strip; sheets of paper

Make a stack of sheets of paper, one for each person present. On the top sheet of paper, draw a large, simple human shape. Cut out all the sheets together.

Everyone can paint thick horizontal stripes down their shape, using two shades of blue. Use the straight end of the card to scrape different patterns into the stripes and then scrape more patterns using the zigzag end of the card, making some straight and some wavy.

Say: God made us all different but his goodness is the same.

 Stick a blue, stripy person in your story book.

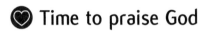 Time to praise God

Hold up a Bible. Explain that the Bible story told us that Jesus is good. Jesus shows us what God is like. God is good.

It tells us in the Bible

You are good to everyone, and you take care of all your creation. (Psalm 145:9)

Make a seated circle. Read the verse aloud, slowly.

Say: I wonder it means to take care of something…

Listen to the children's answers.

Say the first phrase to the person on your left and ask them to repeat it to the person on their left, and so on, until it returns to you. The second phrase is sent around the circle in the same direction. Finally, the Bible reference and a Bible are passed around and returned to you.

Music praise

You can sing together or along with a CD or DVD. Some children may prefer to do actions, dance or jump around rather than sing. Alternatively, you can play a CD while doing the Bible verse activity. Choose songs relating to God's goodness (see page 19 for suggested CDs).

Activity options

1. Blue for you!

Bring: Blue playdough; blue felt-tipped pen; large sheet of paper

Bubble-write the words 'God is good' in large letters. Using playdough, shape letters over the phrase.

2. God is good!

Bring: Dark blue and light blue paper; blue crayons or felt-tipped pens

Share an appropriate example of personal illness, when God showed his goodness to you. Using a blue pen, write it briefly on the light blue paper and tear it out. Everyone can do the same. Stick the examples of God's goodness on to the dark blue paper.

Say: We can praise God for his goodness to us.

Save the sheet for your prayer time.

 Stick the sheet in your story book later.

Discover other people's stories

Choose from the options below to discover people who were (or are) inspired to show God's goodness.

Tell their story and discuss how they show God's goodness through their actions.

- Peter and John took the opportunity to heal a lame man. Find the story below.
- Naaman's servant told her master about God's prophet. Find the story in your Bible: 2 Kings 5:1–15 or a children's Bible storybook such as *Barnabas Children's Bible*, Nos. 178 and 179.

- Paul Brant: a doctor who spent his life caring for leprosy patients. Find his story in *Ten Boys Who Used their Talents* by Irene Howat.
- Leprosy Mission: an organisation relieving and supporting those with leprosy today. See www.leprosymission.org.uk.
- Mercy Ships: a Christian organisation bringing medicine and surgery to people in need. See www.mercyships.org.uk.
- Focus on a local person or organisation that shows God's goodness.

Find Peter and John's story in Acts 3:1–10; *Barnabas Children's Bible*, No. 320.

Bring: Blue craft sticks or strips of card (two per person)

Every time the word 'extra-ordinary' is used in the story, everyone can cross their two craft sticks in the air.

It was an ordinary day—just like every other ordinary day. Every ordinary day since he could remember, the man had been carried to sit outside the temple. He had never been able to walk and couldn't work like other people. He begged for money from people going in and out of the temple. Everyone knew him. Every ordinary day they had seen him there, begging.

But this was not an ordinary day. This was an extra-ordinary day. This extra-ordinary day, Peter and John came to the temple to pray. This extra-ordinary day, the man asked them to give him some money. This extra-ordinary day, Peter said to him, 'We don't have any money but, in the name of Jesus Christ of Nazareth, walk!' This extra-ordinary day, Peter helped the man stand up. This extra-ordinary day, the man felt his legs and ankles become strong. This extra-ordinary day, the man jumped right up and walked. Extra-ordinary!

The man followed Peter and John into the temple, walking and jumping and praising God very loudly for his goodness. Extra-ordinary! Everyone who saw him was amazed. They knew who he was. He had never been able to walk. Extra-ordinary!

Consider Peter and John's story

- What did we find out about Peter and John in that story?
- I wonder what the man did the next day, and the next day…
- Peter and John showed God's goodness to a man who needed it.
- All goodness comes from God and he wants us to share it with others.

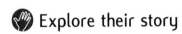 Explore their story

Choose one or more activity, depending on your group and time.

1. Senses poem

Children might like to create or use a senses poem based on your chosen character's experiences. Help them write a line for each sense and put them together to make a poem, rhymed or freestyle. For example:

The ground is hard and stony, the sun hot on my back. (Touch)
The donkeys wait so patiently for yet another sack. (Smell)
The dust kicked up around me lies thickly in my throat. (Taste)
The children run past, laughing, as they chase a poor old goat. (See)
The singing from the temple is tuneful, sweet and loud. (Hearing)
If I could walk in through the door, then I would feel so proud. (Feelings)

 Stick the poem in your story book.

2. Moving all over!

Sing the action rhyme 'One finger, one thumb, keep moving'.

One finger, one thumb, keep moving (x 3), we'll all be merry and bright.
One finger, one thumb, one arm, keep moving (x 3), we'll all be merry and bright.
One finger, one thumb, one arm, one leg, keep moving (x 3),
we'll all be merry and bright.
One finger, one thumb, one arm, one leg, one nod of the head, keep moving (x 3),
we'll all be merry and bright.
One finger, one thumb, one arm, one leg, one nod of the head, stand up, sit down,
keep moving (x 3), we'll all be merry and bright.

3. Playtime

Younger children can have a time of free play. If possible, include toys and puzzles that reflect the idea of showing goodness to those who are unwell, such as a doctor's kit and soft toys, play people in hospital and so on.

 Respond

You may like to play a worship CD quietly in the background during this activity.

What about me?

Say: What do you think it means to show goodness? Do you know that God wants us to show his goodness? I would like to show God's goodness and be like *[the character in your chosen story]*. Would you like to show God's goodness? I wonder what we could do that would show God's goodness…

Listen to the children's ideas, share your own and help them form some practical possibilities. Write them on a blue craft stick or strip of card to take home.

Let's pray

Help children to contribute specific ideas for prayer, using the following pointers. Ask them if there is anything else they would like the group to pray for, referring to the blue sheet of paper from the praise activities if appropriate.

- Let's thank God for his goodness to us, especially when we are hurt or unwell.
- We can ask God to show us others who need his goodness.
- When we are selfish or forgetful, we can tell God we are sorry.

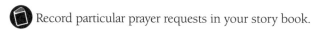 Record particular prayer requests in your story book.

Review

Look back through your story book. Check where today's Bible stories fit in relation to others already in the book. Look at some previous prayer requests and find out if and how they have been answered. Note any answered prayers in the story book.

Way out

Give everyone a blue plaster to put around a finger. In turn, each person can ring the bell and say aloud, 'God is good!'

Family follow-up

See www.barnabasinchurches.org.uk/extra-resources/ to download the family follow-up sheet.

Play

Fill a pastry case with blueberries. Sprinkle with a little sugar. Make meringue and pile it on top of the blueberries. Brown the meringue in the oven or under a grill. See and taste God's goodness!

Play a game of 'Operation', remembering to thank God for his goodness to us.

Gather blue card and craft materials to make 'get well' cards. Keep until needed.

Add 'good' to your 'God is…' collage or patchwork.

Praise

When you eat together, sing the Bible verse rhyme below from Psalm 145:9. Try to sing it as a round to the tune 'Row, row, row the boat'.

Know, know God is good,
The Bible tells us so!
He takes care of all he's made,
That's so good to know!

Use magnetic letters to write the word 'goodness' on the fridge as a family reminder of God's goodness.

The theme colour is blue. Using blue bubble bath or shower gel can act as reminders that we are surrounded by and immersed in God's goodness.

Plan

Explore one or more of the stories together.

When you're out and about, look for people who are showing God's goodness to others. We are all made in God's image and bear his likeness, whether we are people of faith or not. At appointments with the medical profession—doctors, nurses, physiotherapists, dentists and so on—remember God's goodness expressed through people, and pray for them.

Make a note of acts of goodness observed at school, college or work. Share them with the rest of the family. Make a vertical blue stripe on a sheet of paper for each act of goodness. How long will it take to fill the paper?

Ask: How can we show God's goodness to others, either as a family or as individuals? Write your ideas horizontally across your sheet of vertical lines.

Pray

Thank God for any specific ways in which he has shown his goodness to the family. Say sorry for particular times when we have not been willing to show his goodness to others. Ask for God's help to show more of his goodness.

＊

God is self-controlled

- Theme: Managing our lives in God's best ways
- Learn from Jesus: Luke 4:1–13
- Bible verse: 'I treasure your word above all else; it keeps me from sinning against you' (Psalm 119:11).
- Discover other people's stories: David; Paul; early-day Salvationists; Oxford martyrs
- Theme colour: Black

Way in

Traffic lights

Bring: Black paper or cloth; blackboard or black paper; red, orange and green chalks

Cover a table with black paper or cloth.

Say: I wonder why we are using the colour black today…

Put the chalks on the table.

Say: I wonder what we could do with these…

Listen and affirm ideas without comment. Use the chalks to write the word 'self-control' on the blackboard.

Say: Self-control means taking hold—taking control—of how we think and feel and of what we do. Using the chalk, make three circles on the blackboard, the top one red, the middle one orange and the bottom one green.

Say: These signs are important for self-control. We will look at them again later.

Learn from Jesus

Luke 4:1–13: Today's story tells of a time when Jesus needed to be self-controlled. Jesus came to carry out God's big plan to save people from their sins. As part of God's plan, Jesus was baptised in the river Jordan by his cousin, John. Afterwards, Jesus went away into the desert to think quietly and to ask God about the next part of his plan.

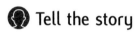 Tell the story

Choose the story option most appropriate for your group.

Some parts of the Judean desert were sandy, some parts rocky, and some parts had bushes, but very few people lived there. It was a great place for Jesus to get away from everyone and everything and to listen to God.

Jesus stayed in the desert for 40 days and 40 nights, and he didn't eat any food during that time. When the devil saw how weak and hungry Jesus was, he tried to get Jesus to make some wrong choices.

The devil said, 'If you're God's Son, tell this stone to turn into bread.' Jesus is all-powerful and could have done that, but he wouldn't use his great power just to feed himself. Jesus used the scriptures to answer the devil. He said, 'No one can live only on food.'

Next, the devil took Jesus to a high place where Jesus could see all the countries of the world laid out in front of him. The devil said, 'I will give all this power and glory to you… Just worship me, and you can have it.' Jesus refused to worship the devil and told him what the scriptures say: 'Worship the Lord your God and serve only him!'

Next, the devil showed Jesus the city of Jerusalem from the top of the temple. The devil said to him, 'If you are God's Son, jump off. The scriptures say that God will tell the angels to take care of you.' Jesus knew that God's power was not to be used like this and he told the devil off: 'The scriptures also say, "Don't try to test the Lord your God!"'

The devil gave up for the time being. Jesus had refused to do what the devil said, because it was wrong. Jesus was very self-controlled.

1. Desert places

Bring: Pebbles

Everyone can make piles of pebbles as you tell the story.

2. Desert journey

As you tell the story, add the following words. Repeat them after the first paragraph and before Jesus' response to each of the three temptations, leading children around your meeting space and acting out the words.

'I expect Jesus walked a while… sat down and thought a while… listened to God a while… talked to God a while… walked a while more… It was important for Jesus to hear God right.'

If you only have young children present, you may prefer to use these additional words after the second sentence, and again after the third sentence, of the following shortened version of the story:

All the time Jesus was in the desert, he didn't eat anything. He was only interested in hearing what God wanted. But the devil didn't want Jesus to do what God wanted. The devil tried his hardest to get Jesus to disobey God. The devil tried and tried, but Jesus said 'no' to the devil every time. Jesus used Bible verses he had learnt and said 'no' to the devil. Jesus was self-controlled.

3. Find the story in the Bible

An adult or child may read Luke 4:1–13 from a Bible or children's Bible storybook such as *Barnabas Children's Bible*, No. 256.

Consider the story

- I wonder how Jesus managed not to give in to the devil…
- I wonder if those ways would work for us, too…
- What did we find out about Jesus in that story?
- In what ways is Jesus is self-controlled, just like God?

✋ Explore the story

Choose one or more of the activities, depending on your group and time.

1. Stop! Wait! Go!

Bring: Three torches; red, orange and green cellophane or sweet wrappers

Cover one torch with red, one with orange and one with green cellophane or sweet wrapper.

Point to the blackboard that you used in the 'Way in' activity.

Say: I wonder what these circles remind us of. What do the different colours mean? When the devil tempts us to do something wrong, this is what we must do…

- Before we do anything, we must STOP. *(Flash the red torch.)*
- Before we do anything, we must WAIT, think about what could happen, and decide what's the right thing to do. *(Flash the orange torch.)*
- Then, when we've made the right choice, we can GO and do the right thing. *(Flash the green torch.)*

Take turns to flash the right torches on STOP, WAIT and GO.

Say: Jesus was very weak and hungry and was tempted by the devil to turn a stone into bread. Jesus had to STOP, WAIT and think, then make the right choice and GO.

Say: Jesus knew that the next part of God's plan would be very, very difficult, and the devil tempted Jesus to take an easier way. Jesus had to STOP, WAIT and think, then make the right choice and GO.

Say: Jesus knew that God could keep him safe from harm, and the devil tempted him to show how special he was. Jesus had to STOP, WAIT and think, then make the right choice and GO.

2. Colour me!

Bring: Black paper; white paper; scissors; red, orange and green felt-tipped pens or crayons

Cut out three white paper circles for everyone. Colour them red, orange and green and stick them in traffic light order on black paper.

Say: When we are tempted to do something we know is wrong, God wants us to STOP, WAIT and think, and then GO and do the right thing.

 Stick a paper traffic light in your story book.

3. Ready reminder

Bring: Lengths of green, orange and red wool.

Knot together one or two strands of each colour of wool. Plait the three colours together. The plaits can be joined up to make a bracelet, used as a bookmark or kept in a pocket or bag as a reminder that we can be self-controlled.

 Fix a 'ready reminder' in your story book.

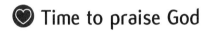 Time to praise God

Hold up a Bible. Explain that the Bible story told us that when Jesus was tempted to do something wrong, he was self-controlled. Jesus shows us what God is like. God is self-controlled.

It tells us in the Bible

I treasure your word above all else; it keeps me from sinning against you (Psalm 119:11).

Bring: 15 pieces of gold card; small lidded gold gift or craft box

Print or write out the Bible verse and reference, one word on each piece of card. Place the pieces of gold card in the gift box and place the lid on the box. In turn, hold the gift box and say aloud the Bible verse. Talk about Jesus knowing and understanding God's word and how it helped him take control of his thoughts and actions.

Music praise

You can sing together or along with a CD or DVD. Some children may prefer to do actions, dance or jump around rather than sing. Alternatively, you can play a CD while doing the Bible verse activity. Choose songs relating to self-control (see page 19 for suggested CDs).

Activity options

1. Pass the parcel

Bring: A 'pass the parcel' game with red, orange and green lollies in the centre and various paper slips, with situations to consider, within the layers. For example:
- Your friends are being unkind to someone at school and you're tempted to join in…
- When others are unkind to you or bully you, you're tempted to hurt them back…
- You want another half-hour on the computer and are tempted to argue…
- You're losing a game and are tempted to cheat…

Play 'pass the parcel' and, at each turn, apply the STOP! WAIT! GO! principle to the situation. Keep the lollies for later.

 Stick the paper slips in your story book and write STOP! WAIT! GO!

2. Hold on tight!

Show the actions for this rhyme and repeat several times, encouraging children to join in.

- STOP: Freeze with hand up, as if stopping traffic.
- WAIT: Freeze, poised and ready to run.
- GO: Run on the spot.

When I'm tempted to do wrong: STOP! WAIT! GO!
I can say this all day long: STOP! WAIT! GO!
To God's word I'll hold on tight. (Fists across heart.)
I can choose to do what's right. (Point four times in front.)
I can walk in God's bright light. (Walk on the spot.)
With STOP! WAIT! GO!

Discover other people's stories

Choose from the options below to discover people who were self-controlled, like God.

Tell their story and discuss how they showed God's self-control through their actions.

- David showed self-control when tempted to kill King Saul. Find the story below.
- Paul left his friends and went steadfastly into an uncertain future. Find the story in your Bible: Acts 21:1–15 or a children's Bible storybook such as *Barnabas Children's Bible*, No. 349.
- Early Salvationists did not retaliate when faced with opposition and danger. Find the story by entering 'Salvation Army opposition and persecution' into an internet search engine.
- Oxford Martyrs were self-controlled even in death. As they burnt to death, Hugh Latimer said to Nicholas Ridley, 'We shall this day light such a candle in England as I trust by God's grace shall never be put out.' Find the story at http://oxford.openguides.org/wiki?Oxford_Martyrs.

Find David's story in 1 Samuel 26; *Barnabas Children's Bible*, No. 126.

Bring: Frieze paper; black felt-tipped pen; red felt-tipped pen

Divide the frieze paper into eight sections. Together, draw simple stick figures as you tell the story. Use a black pen for David and a red pen for everyone else.

1. David ran away. He hid in a cave with his friends because King Saul wanted to kill him.
2. King Saul took 3000 soldiers to try to find David.
3. One dark night, David took his friend, Abishai, to find King Saul, and they crept quietly to the king's camp.
4. King Saul's bodyguard was nowhere to be seen. King Saul was asleep in his tent, with his spear and water jug nearby.
5. Abishai wanted to kill King Saul but David said, 'No.' Instead, they picked up the spear and water jug and left.
6. When they were safely away, David shouted out loud to King Saul's bodyguard, 'What are you doing? You're supposed to be looking after the king! Where's his spear and water jug?'
7. The bodyguard knew that David had been in King Saul's tent and that David could have killed the king if he had wanted to.
8. King Saul woke up and shouted back to David, 'Thank you for not killing me.'

Consider David's story

- What did we find out about David in that story?
- I wonder what might have happened if David had killed King Saul…
- David's self-control came from God.
- God wants us to be self-controlled, too.

Explore their story

Choose one or more of the activities, depending on your group and time.

1. Jump to it!

Say: People often talk about 'exercising self-control'.

Do some simple exercises together, such as star jumps, running on the spot, lunges and press-ups.

Between the types of exercise, *Say:* When we exercise our muscles, they grow stronger, and exercise gets easier. When we exercise self-control, it grows stronger, and self-control gets easier. We don't have to exercise self-control on our own. God will help us when we ask him. *[Name your chosen character]* knew the right thing to do, and he was self-controlled.

2. Flower power

> **Bring:** Newspapers; sticky tape

Roll up a newspaper and use sticky tape to fix the tube. From the top, make vertical cuts to about a third of the way down. Gently push from the bottom and the 'flower' should sprout out from the top. Help children make their own flowers.

Say: Self-control grows and flowers when we use it.

3. Playtime

Younger children can have a time of free play. If possible, include toys and puzzles that encourage children to show self-control, such as road safety with cars and play people, or playing shops and a shopping trip.

♥ Respond

You may like to play a worship CD quietly in the background during this activity.

What about me?

Say: What do you think it means to be self-controlled? Do you know that God wants us to be self-controlled, like him? I would like to be self-controlled like God, and be like *[the character in your chosen story]*. Would you like to be self-controlled? I wonder when we might need to be self-controlled…

Listen to the children's ideas and share your own. Those who wish to do so can hold the gold gift box with the Bible verse and share their ideas aloud. At the end, open the lid, take out the cards and sort them to display the verse.

Let's pray

Help children to contribute specific ideas for prayer, using the following pointers. Ask them if there is anything else they would like the group to pray for.

- Let's thank God that he is always self-controlled.
- Sometimes we're not self-controlled like God, and we can tell him that we're sorry.
- Sometimes it's hard to be self-controlled like God, and we need to ask him to help us.

 Record particular prayer requests in your story book.

Review

Look back through your story book. Check where today's Bible stories fit in relation to others already in the book. Look at some previous prayer requests and find out if and how they have been answered. Note any answered prayers in the story book.

Way out

> **Bring:** Black fabric

Have everyone hold the black fabric taut between them.
    Say: Self-control means being firm and strong, choosing right with God's help. Give out the lollies.

Family follow-up

See www.barnabasinchurches.org.uk/extra-resources/ to download the family follow-up sheet.

Play

Research volcanoes and think about how they illustrate a destructive force that is like lack of self-control.

Children are constantly developing new motor skills, learning to control their bodies: colouring a picture within the lines, writing neatly, balancing on a bike, accurately kicking a ball, and so on. Praise achievement and use it as a reminder that we can control our minds and behaviour, too.

Play a game of Snap. As you play, take the opportunity to talk about cheating, sulking or giving up, and point out that when we are tempted to do those things, at that moment we can choose what we will do next and take time to make a right choice. That's called self-control.

Add 'self-control' to your 'God is…' collage or patchwork.

Praise

Make 15 circles from red, orange and green paper. Write one word of the Bible verse plus reference on each of them. Together, stick the words in the correct order on a sheet of black paper. Talk about STOP! WAIT! GO!

Use magnetic letters to write the word 'self-control' on the fridge, as a family reminder to make right choices when tempted to do wrong.

The theme colour is black. Buying or picking blackberries to make a blackberry and apple crumble, tucking a few black grapes into lunchboxes, or adding black olives to a favourite pizza can act as a reminder to be self-controlled.

Plan

Explore one or more of the stories together.

Ask: 'What can we do as a family, or as individuals, to become more self-controlled?' Discuss particular areas of temptation—for example, losing temper, lying, watching or playing some TV, DVD or computer games. Talk about what might replace those TV programmes or games if we choose not to watch or play them. The black screen of the switched-off TV or computer can be a sign of self-control being exercised.

Jesus used scripture verses to say 'No' to the devil. Make a family search for short, helpful verses, such as Proverbs 25:28.

Pray

Thank God for any specific ways in which he has helped anyone in the family to become more self-controlled. Say sorry to God for particular times when self-control has not been exercised. Ask for God's help in named times of temptation.

✳

God is peace

- **Theme:** Being a peacemaker, like Jesus
- **Learn from Jesus:** Luke 22:47–54
- **Bible verse:** 'I give you peace, the kind of peace that only I can give' (John 14:27).
- **Discover other people's stories:** Abram; Jacob and Esau; Elisabeth Elliot; United Nations; NCPO
- **Theme colour:** Light blue

Way in

Friends together!

> **Bring:** Light blue paper or cloth; a picture of a group of smiling people; light blue felt-tipped pen

Cover a table with light blue paper or cloth.

Say: I wonder why we are using a light blue colour today...

Show the picture.

Say: I wonder why we are looking at these people today...

Listen and affirm ideas without comment. Turn the picture over and write the five letters of the word 'peace' across the back. Tear the picture into five pieces, one letter per piece.

Say: Sometimes people argue and fall out, and are not friends any more. These people need someone to be a peacemaker. I wonder what 'peacemaker' means...

Listen to ideas without comment. Save paper pieces until the end of the session.

Learn from Jesus

Luke 22:47–54: Today's story is about Jesus being a peacemaker. Soon Jesus would be arrested and killed as part of God's big plan. Jesus had been praying in a garden while his friends slept, asking God to make him strong to face the pain that was coming.

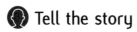 Tell the story

Choose the story option most appropriate for your group.

Jesus waited for the soldiers to come and take him away. (*Shade eyes.*)
   Jesus wouldn't fight the soldiers. (*Hands up in surrender.*)
   He wouldn't let his friends fight them, either. (*Hand out as a stop sign.*)
   Jesus was doing what God wanted. (*Hands out to God.*)
   His friends didn't understand what was happening. (*Shrug shoulders.*)
   Can you hear them? Stamp, stamp, stamp.
   Soldiers coming. Tramp, tramp, tramp.
   Run and hide, Jesus! Oh, no! They're here.
   'Leave him alone!' his friends shouted, wanting to fight. (*Push hands away.*)
   'I'll fight them, Jesus!' (*Fist-fight actions.*)
   'Don't let them take you!' (*Shake head.*)
   Too late. He's gone with them. (*Hold head in hands.*)

1. Copy me!

Everyone can copy your actions as you tell the story.

2. Colour of peace

> **Bring:** Light blue paper

Say: There may be times when good people need to fight for what is right, but, after the fighting is finished, peace still needs to be made between the two sides and it's not easy. Sometimes it is better to be brave and refuse to fight in the first place, like Jesus. That's a very tough thing to do.

Say: What shape do you think peace might be?

As you read the story without the actions, everyone can use the light blue paper to draw their chosen shape for peace.

 Stick peace shapes in your story book.

3. Find the story in the Bible

An adult or child may read Luke 22:47–54 from a Bible or children's Bible storybook such as *Barnabas Children's Bible*, No. 305.

Consider the story

- I wonder what the soldiers thought might happen when they came to arrest Jesus…
- I wonder why Jesus didn't let his friends fight for him…
- What did we find out about Jesus in that story?
- Jesus is a peacemaker, just like God.

Explore the story

Choose one or more of the activities, depending on your group and time.

1. Freeze-frame

Bring: A camera

Use both hands, L-shaped, to 'frame' your face. Choose one moment in the story. Decide how the various characters might feel at that moment. Everyone can make a photo frame with their hands and freeze the expression of their character. For example, as the soldiers arrive:

- Jesus: waiting calmly
- Jesus' friends: shocked; angry and ready to fight
- Soldiers: fierce; determined

Take photographs to be printed out later.

If you wish to do so, stick photographs in your story book, with captions explaining the expressions.

2. Perfect peace

Bring: Light blue fabric

Lie or sit on the floor. Waft the light blue fabric gently over everyone.

Say: Some people want peace to just happen quietly, gently, in a relaxing way, calm and still. But peace has to be made and then kept.

Run around carefully, avoiding each other and the furniture.

Say: Making peace can be hard work. Even when we think we've made peace, we have to keep watching out for things that can break the peace again.

Stop running.

Say: Only Jesus can bring lasting, perfect peace.

3. Peace bridge

Bring: Construction bricks; three play people

Together, build a bridge eleven bricks long.

Say: When friends or families fall out and want to fight, or countries go to war, a peacemaker is needed. A peacemaker can build a bridge between people, stand in the middle, try to sort out the reasons for the fight and help everyone to be at peace again.

Place a figure at the bridge centre as the peacemaker. Move the other two figures gradually towards the centre.

Say: The first step is for both sides to calm down.

The second step is for each to say how they feel.

The third step is for both to listen to each other.

The fourth step is for both of them to decide how things could be better again.

The fifth step is to agree to meet halfway and say sorry (*remove peacemaker*).

The sixth step is to try again and practise being friends.

Say: Jesus can bring lasting peace between friends, families and countries, and Jesus makes peace between us and God.

♥ Time to praise God

Hold up a Bible. Explain that the Bible story told us that Jesus is a peacemaker.
Jesus shows us what God is like. God is peace.

It tells us in the Bible

'I give you peace, the kind of peace that only I can give.' (John 14:27)

> Bring: Copies of the United Nations flag

Give everyone a copy of the UN flag.

Say: Lots of people and organisations, like the United Nations, work hard for
peace in countries all across the world.

Have everyone hold the flags high over their heads. Bring the flags down
slowly until they rest on your heads.

Say: Jesus said, 'I give you peace, the kind of peace that only I can give.'
God's peace is the best peace of all. Jesus came to bring us God's peace. Only
God's peace can last.

Write the Bible verse across the flags. Keep them for later.

 Stick a flag in your story book.

Music praise

You can sing together or along with a CD or DVD. Some children may prefer to
do actions, dance or jump around rather than sing. Alternatively, you can play
a CD while doing the Bible verse activity. Choose songs relating to God's peace
(see page 19 for suggested CDs).

Activity options

1. Peace chant

Stand everyone in a circle, facing left. Have one person (X) facing the other way.
X shakes the right hand of the person facing them (Y) and moves on, shaking

everyone's hand until they return to their start position, where they rejoin the circle facing left.

Once X has shaken Y's hand, Y turns round and starts the same process, shaking hands round the circle. Continue until everyone has walked round the circle, shaking hands with everyone else.

Repeat, adding the chant: 'P-E-A-C-E, P-E-A-C-E, P-E-A-C-E, peace Jesus gives me.'

2. Perfect peace

Bring: Light blue crêpe paper, cut into streamers

Sing the song slowly to the tune 'Pop goes the weasel' and wave the streamers, making figures of eight and wide circles.

Praise you, Jesus, for your peace.
Praise you, praise you, Jesus.
Only you can make real peace,
Peace that can last.

Discover other people's stories

Choose from the options below to discover people who were (or are) inspired to be peacemakers, like God.

 Tell their story and discuss how they show God's peace through their actions.

- Abram: a man who would not fight and kept the peace in his family. Find the story below.
- Jacob and Esau: brothers who fell out and, after long years, were reconciled. Find the story in your Bible: Genesis 33:1–15 or a children's Bible storybook such as *Barnabas Children's Bible*, No. 28.
- Elisabeth Elliot: Elisabeth went in peace to live with the tribe that had murdered her husband. Find her story in *Ten Girls Who Made History* by Irene Howat (Christian Focus Publications, 2007).
- Network of Christian Peace Organisations: www.ncpo.org.uk.

- United Nations: www.un.org/en/peacekeeping.
- Focus on a local person, someone in your church, or an organisation with peacekeeping or mediation skills.

Find Abram's story in Genesis 13; *Barnabas Children's Bible*, No. 12

Bring: Lily-of-the-valley scented soap; bowl of water; towel

Say: This soap is scented with a flower called lily of the valley. Lilies are sometimes known as flowers of peace.

At the end of each paragraph in the story, let everyone wash their hands and smell the scent.

Long ago, in biblical times, God was guiding Abram and his wife, Sarai, to a new country. They took Abram's nephew with them, along with all their flocks and herds of animals and many servants and herdsmen. Abram's nephew was called Lot. They travelled with the animals, living in tents and moving on when fresh grass was needed. Abram trusted God to show him the way to the new country.

The servants and herdsmen sometimes argued and fell out with each other. Abram and Lot didn't always agree, either. Abram needed to be a peacemaker.

Eventually, God told Abram they had arrived at the new country. It was beautiful. But again, the servants and herdsmen began to argue over the water and whose animals were more important. Then Lot tried to argue with Abram about how to share the land and the water. Abram needed to be a peacemaker.

Abram said to Lot, 'Don't let's fall out. There is so much land. You choose where you want to live, and I'll go somewhere else.' As Abram was head of the family, he should have chosen first, but he let Lot choose first. Lot looked at the new country and he chose the best land for his animals.

Abram didn't argue with Lot. He chose to keep the peace. Abram took Sarai, his herds and flocks and servants and herdsmen, and went to live in another part of the new country, thanking God for his goodness.

Consider Abram's story

- What did we find out about Abram in that story?
- I wonder how Abram felt when Lot chose the best place to live…
- I wonder what makes a good peacemaker…
- Abram was a peacemaker.

 Stick the soap wrapper in your story book.

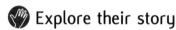 Explore their story

Choose one or more of the activities, depending on your group and time.

1. Hum the peace

Make a seated circle. Check that everyone knows how to hum.

Say: We're going to hum one long note together, taking breaths at different times so that the hum doesn't stop.

Practise a few times and then try to sustain it for two minutes without breaking the sound.

Say: It's hard to keep a hum going without letting it break down. Sometimes it's hard to keep friends and family and countries going without letting them break down. But Jesus will help us make peace if we ask him to.

2. Think about it

Bring: A large sheet of paper, light blue felt-tipped pens

Encourage the children to think about your chosen story, building up a picture and answering questions. Using paper and light blue felt-tipped pens, bubble-write ideas over a large sheet of paper and colour or pattern them to match the word. For example:

Abram's and Lot's journey was taking years, mostly through wild, deserted places. Abram kept saying that God knew where he was taking them. Did Lot always believe him? No map. No satnav. Just God. How do you think Abram felt? How do you think Lot felt?

Every time they all stopped to make camp, the tents had to be put up, and people and animals fed and watered. What made a good place to stop and stay for a while? (*Examples: water and good grazing.*)

What things might have made them worried along the journey? (*Examples: wild animals, long distances between water sources, running out of food.*)

What things might have made Lot angry or argumentative? (*Examples: which direction they took, how much longer it was going to take, who should have the best grazing.*)

What things might have gone wrong on the journey? (*Examples: servants grumbling, people and animals getting sick, the people who lived in the land being unwelcoming.*)

Say: It wasn't easy for Abram to make and keep the peace, but God helped him.

3. Playtime

Younger children can have a time of free play. If possible, include toys and puzzles that need to be shared. Encourage children to take turns.

♥ Respond

You may like to play a worship CD quietly in the background during this activity.

What about me?

Say: What do you think it means to be a peacemaker? Do you know that God is peace and wants us to be peacemakers, like him? I would like to be a peacemaker like God, and be like *[the character in your chosen story]*. Would you like to be a peacemaker? I wonder what we could do that would help to bring peace around us…

Listen to children's ideas, share your own and help them form some practical possibilities. Ideas can be written on the back of their UN flag and taken home.

Let's pray

Help children to contribute specific ideas for prayer, using the following pointers. Ask them if there are any others they would like the group to pray for.

- Let's thank God that he is peace, and a peacemaker.
- Sometimes we cause trouble instead of being peacemakers. We can tell God we are sorry.
- Sometimes it's hard to be a peacemaker. We can ask God to help us.

 If you wish to do so, record particular prayer requests in your story book.

Review

Look back through your story book. Check where today's Bible stories fit in relation to others already in the book. Look at some previous prayer requests and find out if and how they have been answered. Note any answered prayers in the story book.

Way out

Bring out the pieces of the photograph from the beginning of the session. Children can help you put the photograph back together.

Say: Remember, only Jesus can bring lasting peace between families, friends and countries.

 Stick the photograph in your story book.

Family follow-up

See www.barnabasinchurches.org.uk/extra-resources/ to download the family follow-up sheet.

Play

Make time to play computer, board or card games together as a family. Competitive games, sharing and turn-taking often present opportunities for peacemaking. Try to be 'peace-aware' and to practise peacemaking. For younger children, make a reward chart to encourage peacemaking efforts. Older children, too, will appreciate helpful comments and a special treat to look forward to.

Find images of the UN flag to print or copy. Note the olive branches on either side of the world, as a symbol of peace around the world. Fix a flag to everyone's bedroom door and write peacemaking ideas on them.

Add 'peace' to your 'God is…' collage or patchwork.

Praise

At meal times, tap out and say aloud the Bible verse together. Remind the family what a wonderful gift peacemaking is among friends, families and countries.

Use magnetic letters to write the verse or just the word 'peace' on the fridge as a family reminder of God's peacemaking abilities.

The theme colour is light blue. In spring time, finding a bluebell wood to lie down in, smelling and breathing in God's peace, is a great way to remember those you know who need God's peace in their lives. Plant some forget-me-not seeds in your garden or windowbox to help you think and pray for them.

Plan

Explore one or more of the stories together.

When you're out and about, look at the ways people treat each other in their words and actions, and how these can escalate to a breakdown of peace. Pray for any difficult situations you observe and ask God to bring his peace and restoration. Share them with the rest of the family and discuss how and when the people concerned might have stepped back or resolved their differences.

Ask: What can we do as a family, or as individuals, to bring God's peace? Look for opportunities in your immediate family, locally and globally to pray and find practical applications for peacemaking.

Pray

Thank God for his peace and for being able to bring his peace to others. Say sorry to God for particular times when peace has been broken or trouble deliberately caused. Look at any current relationship issues or difficulties and ask God for peacemaking skills to help make restoration.

＊

God is trustworthy

- Theme: Trusting God with everything in life
- Learn from Jesus: Matthew 6:25–34
- Bible verse: 'Lord All-Powerful, you are God. You have promised me some very good things, and you can be trusted to do what you promise' (2 Samuel 7:28).
- Discover other people's stories: Hannah; Noah; George Müller; John Bunyan
- Theme colour: Brown

Way in

Trust me!

Bring: Brown paper or cloth; birdseed

Cover a table with brown paper or cloth.

Say: I wonder why we are using the colour brown today…

Put the birdseed on the table.

Say: I wonder what we could do with this…

Listen and affirm ideas without comment.

Say: If I ask you to fall backwards, can you trust me to catch you?

If anyone trusts you, demonstrate by catching them.

Say: Sometimes people let us down, forget promises or don't do what they say, and it can be hard to trust them again. We're like that, too, making it hard for others to trust us. Only God is truly trustworthy. We can trust him with our lives.

Learn from Jesus

Matthew 6:25–34: Today's story is about Jesus telling us not to worry about anything because God is trustworthy. As Jesus looked at the crowd of people all around him, he could see that they were worried about all kinds of things.

🎭 Tell the story

Choose the story option most appropriate for your group.

Jesus had grown up in his family and in his town and knew what people worried about: earning enough money to live, crops failing, being ill… Jesus knew that the people listening to him were worried and had forgotten that God could be trusted to take care of them.

Jesus said, 'The life God's given you is more important than all those things that worry you. Look at the birds. They don't fly about, worrying over the harvest, because God our Father feeds them. If they're valuable to God, don't you think you're even more valuable? And then you worry about clothes and what to wear. Look at the lilies, other flowers and grasses in the fields. God's made them so beautiful! The richest person ever couldn't look better than these. Flowers soon fade and die. If God takes care of things that only last such a short while, don't you think he can be trusted to take care of you? So stop worrying! God our Father knows exactly what you need. Look to God first of all and keep him in the most important place. He will give you everything you need.'

1. Just trust

> **Bring:** A large sheet of paper; finger paints; wipes; photo images of wild flowers and birds; a camera

Create a bird and flower poster, filling it with a riot of colour. Finger-paint birds with brown paint, laying two fingers in paint for bird bodies, hands for wings, and fingertips for heads and tails. Paint flowers in multi-colours. Use wipes in between colours. Tell the story while everyone paints.

Show photo images of wild flowers and birds. Compare with the poster.

Say: Our poster is excellent, but photographs are a more trustworthy image of flowers and birds. God can be trusted to look after the flowers and birds, and we can trust him to look after us.

 Take a photograph of the poster and print it out for your story book.

2. What a buzz!

Say: If worry has a sound, what do you think it might sound like?

Listen to ideas. Example: a swarm of bees buzzing inside our head.

Say: If trust has a sound, what do you think it might sound like?

Listen to ideas. Example: a baby bird cheeping while it waits for its mother to feed it.

Tell the story, stopping to insert chosen sounds for worry, and chosen sounds for trusting God.

3. Find the story in the Bible

An adult or child may read Matthew 6:25–34 from a Bible or children's Bible storybook such as *Barnabas Children's Bible*, No. 264.

Consider the story

- I wonder why crowds of people came to listen to Jesus…
- I wonder what we might have been worrying about if we had been there…
- What did we find out about Jesus in that story?
- In what ways is Jesus trustworthy, just like God?

Explore the story

Choose one or more of the activities, depending your group and time.

1. Weight of worries

Bring: Balance scales with weights or scales and some heavy objects; squares of brown paper

Everyone thinks of something they or their parents are worried about: tests, bullies, peer pressure, money, job, health and so on.

Say: We sometimes say that worries 'weigh heavy on our minds'. How much do you think your worry might weigh?

Everyone chooses a weight or heavy object. Write the worries on squares of paper.

Say: When God is the most important person in our lives, we can trust him to take care of us and give us what we need. He can take the weight off our mind. Writing our worry on the paper is like trusting it to God.

Compare the weight of the paper with the heavy weights.

 If you wish to do so, stick the worries in your story book.

2. Light as a feather!

Bring: Craft feathers; newspapers

Fold sheets of newspaper to make a bat for everyone. Give each person a feather to place on a start line, well spaced out. Flap the bats behind the feathers (without touching them) to try to get them to the finish line.

Say: If feathers were heavy, birds wouldn't be able to fly. Things that worry us can be as light as a feather if we trust God to take care of us and give us what we need.

 If you wish to do so, stick a feather in your story book.

3. Buzz wire

Bring: A buzz wire game

Take turns to play the game.

Say: When we worry, it's like a buzz in the brain. God wants us to relax and trust him with everything in life.

♥ Time to praise God

Hold up a Bible. Explain that the Bible story told us that God is trustworthy. Jesus shows us what God is like. God is trustworthy.

It tells us in the Bible

'Lord All-Powerful, you are God. You have promised me some very good things, and you can be trusted to do what you promise.' (2 Samuel 7:28)

> **Bring:** Brown paper with 'trustworthy' written in large outline letters; table; brown tablecloth or paper big enough to cover the table; glue; birdseed

Cover the table with the cloth or paper, and place the smaller sheet of brown paper on top. Cover the letters with glue and pour bird seed on to them. Gently shake loose seeds on to the paper or cloth beneath, and keep it aside for the 'Way out' activity.

Sit in a circle and, if children have made the 'Just trust' bird and flower poster (p. 104), place it on the floor in the centre. Repeat the Bible verse, phrase by phrase.

Music praise

You can sing together or along with a CD or DVD. Some children may prefer to do actions, dance or jump around rather than sing. Alternatively, you can play a CD while doing the Bible verse activity. Choose songs relating to God's trustworthiness (see page 19 for suggested CDs).

Activity options

1. Trustworthy God!

> **Bring:** Playdough in assorted colours

Create birds and flowers from the playdough, possibly copying from the pictures used in the story time.

Say: No matter how hard we try, we can't make our birds and flowers look like the ones God makes. We can praise God because he makes everything exactly right, every time. God is trustworthy.

2. No matter what!

Make a circle, touching hands. Everyone says the 'Trust in God' lines below. The leader says the other lines. On the last line, everybody holds hands firmly and leans back as you shout the words, 'A great big lot!' Repeat and have everyone join in shouting the last line.

All: Trust in God…
Leader: when times are easy.
All: Trust in God…
Leader: when times are bad.
All: Trust in God…
Leader: when we feel queasy.
All: Trust in God…
Leader: when we feel sad.
All: Trust in God…
Leader: no matter what.
All: Trust in God…
(Shout together): A great big lot!

Discover other people's stories

Choose from the options below to discover people who were trustworthy, like God.

Tell their story and discuss how they show God's trustworthiness through their actions.

- Hannah trusted God to answer her prayers for a baby. Find the story below.
- Noah trusted God and followed his instructions exactly. Find the story in your Bible: Genesis 6—9 or a children's Bible storybook such as *Barnabas Children's Bible*, Nos. 6–8.

- George Müller: a man who founded an orphanage and discovered God to be completely trustworthy. Find his story in *Ten Boys Who Changed the World* by Irene Howat, or www.mullers.org.
- John Bunyan: imprisoned for his faith, John found God to be trustworthy. Find his story on Torchlighters *Heroes of the Faith* DVD.
- Focus on someone in your church, a local person or organisation who shows trust in God.

Find Hannah's story in 1 Samuel 1:1–20; *Barnabas Children's Bible* No. 107.

> **Bring:** A small tree branch with three or more other branches on it; brown wool

As you begin the story, start to weave the wool randomly through and around the branches. Pass it to others to do the same as the story continues, ensuring that everyone has a turn.

Hannah lived in biblical times, long ago. Hannah had a husband who loved her. Hannah had a comfortable house to live in. But Hannah was very unhappy because she wanted a baby. Ages passed but there was still no baby for Hannah. There were other children in the family, but no baby for Hannah.

Hannah went to worship God and pray. Hannah told God how unhappy she was and asked God for a baby of her own. Hannah got very upset, and Eli the priest thought she was drunk until Hannah told him her sadness and her prayers. Eli asked God to answer her prayers and to bless her.

Hannah went home to wait, trusting God to answer her prayers—and he did. When Hannah's baby was born, she thanked God with all her heart. (*Hold up the branch.*) Hannah's life had felt in a tangle, but she trusted God to make things right—and he did. God is trustworthy.

Consider Hannah's story

- What did we find out about Hannah in that story?
- I wonder how Hannah felt when she went home after speaking with Eli...
- Hannah trusted God, and found God to be trustworthy.

✋ Explore their story

Choose one or more of the activities, depending on your group and time.

1. Paint it brown!

Bring: Paints in a range of colours; paintbrushes; water pots; saucers

If you made a flowers and bird poster, display it and talk about the different colours.

Say: God created colours in light to make the world a beautiful place. We can trust God that red is always red. He isn't suddenly going to change the red glow of sunset to green. We can trust God that green is green. He isn't suddenly going to change green grass to blue. If we mix all these paint colours together, what colour will we always get?

Everybody can have a brush to dip in the different colours, washing the brush between each colour, and mixing them on their saucer.

Say: No matter how many times we mix the paints, they will always make brown. God is trustworthy. Like *[name your chosen character]*, we can trust God with everything in life.

2. Emotional times

Bring: Brown fabric

Choose someone to play the role of your chosen character, and place the brown fabric over their shoulders. Ask this person to walk slowly round the room as you retell the story, stopping to think of the emotions they must have felt at key points. Everyone else can represent those emotions, trying to divert the person from their walk. Each time, he or she wraps the brown fabric closely round their shoulders and walks on. For example:

Hannah travelled with lots of happy people. How do you think she felt? 'Sadness' and 'loneliness' might have swallowed Hannah up (*everyone opens their arms wide around Hannah*), but, although Hannah felt sad and lonely, she just kept trusting God.

After offering her own prayers and hearing Eli's prayers, how do you think Hannah felt on the way home? 'Hopeful' and 'excited' might have filled her mind with thoughts of the coming baby (*everyone jumps around Hannah, rocking a baby in their arms*), but, although Hannah was hopeful and excited, she just kept trusting God.

3. Playtime

Younger children can have a time of free play. If possible, include toys and puzzles that can always be trusted to be the same, such as jigsaw trays, memory game cards and so on.

 Respond

You may like to play a worship CD quietly in the background during this activity.

What about me?

> Bring: Brown paper; pencils

Everyone draws around their hand and cuts out the shape.

Say: What do you think it means to be trustworthy? Do you know that God wants us to trust him with everything in life? I would like to trust God with everything in my life, and be like *[the character in your chosen story]*. Would you like to trust God with everything in your life? I wonder what we could do that would show we want to trust God with everything...

Listen to the children's ideas, share your own and help them form some possibilities. Help children to write one idea on their hand to take home.

Say: We can safely put everything in our lives into God's hands and trust him to care for us.

Let's pray

Help children to contribute specific ideas for prayer, using the following pointers. Ask them if there is anything else they would like the group to pray for.

- Let's thank God that he is trustworthy.
- Sometimes we forget how great God is and how much he cares for us.
- Sometimes we start to worry and need to trust him again.

 Record particular prayer requests in your story book.

Review

Look back through your story book. Check where today's Bible stories fit in relation to others already in the book. Look at some previous prayer requests and find out if and how they have been answered. Note any answered prayers in the story book.

Way out

Take the cloth or paper with the excess seeds on it outside to an open space. Shake it up in the air.

Say: If God cares about the birds and feeds them, how much more will he care for us? We can always trust God.

Family follow-up

See www.barnabasinchurches.org.uk/extra-resources/ to download the family follow-up sheet.

Play

Use a bird book to help identify visitors to your garden or local park. Make a birdtable or hang a feeder on a tree or from a balcony or window.

In spring or summer, plant night-scented stock seeds in a tub by the front or back door. When they are grown, their evening perfume can remind everyone that we don't have to worry but can trust God for our needs.

Add 'trustworthy' to your 'God is...' collage or patchwork.

Praise

Choose a simple ringtone from a mobile phone and write some words to fit it, about trusting God. Have everyone change their ringtone to that one. Whenever it rings, you can remember that God is trustworthy.

Write out the Bible verse on several pieces of brown paper, three or four words on each piece. Tuck them into shoes. As the family go in and out of the house, in whatever mood or state, God's words go with them and he is trustworthy.

The theme colour is brown. Using multigrain or seeded bread or rolls for lunchboxes, counting brown birds in the garden or making a chocolate cake or cookies can act as a reminder that God is trustworthy.

Plan

Explore one or more of the stories together.

When you're out and about, find a really muddy place. Put on boots and squelch through the mud, remembering that brown is the colour for God's trustworthiness. Find out about bird reserves (see www.rspb.org.uk/reserves) and plan a special visit to marvel at the diversity of bird-life sustained by God, especially in spring and autumn as birds migrate.

Ask: What can we do as a family or as individuals to learn to trust God more? Look for areas where worry is strong and trust is weak. Read together a biography of a Christian who trusted God in difficult circumstances.

Pray

Name some ways in which God cares for the family, and affirm trust in him. Say sorry to God for particular times when trust has not been given. Determine together to trust God in any particularly challenging situations. Ask God for his help.

*

God is kind

- Theme: We can show God's kindness to those in need
- Learn from Jesus: John 6:1–15
- Bible verse: 'I will tell about the kind deeds the Lord has done. They deserve praise!' (Isaiah 63:7).
- Discover other people's stories: Ruth and Boaz; David; Tearfund; Water Aid; Florence Nightingale
- Theme colour: Green

Way in

Share with me!

Bring: Green paper or cloth; a green apple; knife; plate

Cover a table with green paper or cloth.

Say: I wonder why we are using the colour green today…

Put the items on the table.

Say: I wonder what we could do with these things…

Listen and affirm ideas, and find the best and kindest way to share the apple between everyone. Cut and share the apple.

Alternatively, if you have access to a kitchen, you could bring the ingredients for cakes or cookies (enough to share with the whole congregation at the end of the service, if practical) and have the children help you prepare them. Put them in the oven and set a timer to remind you to take them out at the appropriate time.

Learn from Jesus

John 6:1–15: Today's story tells of a time when Jesus was kind to people who were hungry. Wherever Jesus went, people followed him. They wanted to see and hear the amazing things he said and did, and sometimes they forgot how long they had been out and how far they were from home.

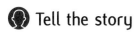 Tell the story

Choose the story option most appropriate for your group.

People walked all around the lake to find Jesus. Even more people came, from all directions. Jesus knew they would be hungry after walking so far to find him. Jesus asked his friend, Philip, if there was anywhere nearby to buy food. Philip shook his head.

One boy had brought a picnic lunch—just some bread and fish—and he offered it to Jesus. Jesus' friends said there wouldn't be enough for everyone, but Jesus told everyone to sit down. Jesus thanked God for the food.

Jesus began to break up the food and his friends shared it out. Jesus kept on breaking up the food, and his friends kept on sharing it out until everyone had had enough to eat. How amazing! Jesus was kind. He didn't want anyone to be hungry.

1. Let's find Jesus!

Begin with everyone standing up. Make up simple actions for everyone as you tell the story.

2. My wonderful day!

Tell the story. Afterwards, make up a group story about the boy who brought his lunch to Jesus, including why he wanted to find Jesus, who prepared his lunch, how he discovered where Jesus was going, how he got there, what he thought about the crowd and about what Jesus said, and what he told his family afterwards.

3. Find the story in the Bible

An adult or child may read John 6:1–15 from a Bible or a children's Bible storybook such as *Barnabas Children's Bible*, No. 275.

Consider the story

- I wonder how people knew where Jesus was going that day...
- I wonder what they thought about the shared lunch...
- What did we find out about Jesus in that story?
- In what ways is Jesus kind, like God?

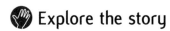 Explore the story

Choose one or more of the activities, depending on your group and time.

1. Aim game!

Bring: Green bucket; green apple

Place the bucket on the floor and stand about two metres away. In turn, try to throw the apple into the bucket. Give several turns.

Say: Some of us are finding this game hard. What would be a kind thing to do, to help?

Invite those who struggle to get the apple in the bucket to stand close enough to reach.

Say: See how battered and bruised this apple is! When people are unkind to us, that's how it makes us feel. God is kind. God wants us to be kind, too, so that we don't make others feel battered or bruised.

2. Kindness collage

Bring: Magazines with pictures of food; other collage materials; four sheets of green paper, each with one of the letters K, I, N, D in large, outline writing

Cut or tear out pictures of food to use with other materials to fill in the letters.

When dry, stick the collage pages in your story book, or photograph them.

3. Apple challenge!

Bring: Green apple; tissues

Place a tissue on the floor. Choose an older volunteer who bends their head down and balances the apple on the back of their neck. The challenge is to try to grab the tissue between their teeth and stand up again without the apple falling off or being touched. Let them have a try.

Say: This is a hard challenge. We can laugh if the apple falls or we can encourage and cheer. What would be the kindest thing to do?

Let your volunteer or someone else try, with kind encouragement. Some children may realise that the kindest thing would be to pick up the tissue and give it to the volunteer!

Time to praise God

Hold up a Bible. Explain that the Bible story told us that Jesus was kind to hungry people. Jesus shows us what God is like. God is kind.

It tells us in the Bible

'I will tell about the kind deeds the Lord has done. They deserve praise!' (Isaiah 63:7)

Say the first part of the Bible verse to an adult helper, with 'speaking hand' actions. Your helper can respond with the second part of the verse, lifting hands in praise. Your helper then says the first part of the verse to someone else, with 'speaking' actions, and they respond with the second part, lifting hands in praise. Continue until everyone has had a turn.

Say: Isaiah *(open hands as a Bible)* 63:7 *(put up six fingers, then three fingers, then seven)*. Then all say the whole verse and reference together, with actions.

Music praise

You can sing together or along with a CD or DVD. Some children may prefer to do actions, dance or jump around rather than sing. Alternatively, you can play a CD while doing the Bible verse activity. Choose songs relating to God's kindness (see page 19 for suggested CDs).

Activity options

1. Sing it out!

Sing the song to the tune 'Twinkle, twinkle, little star'.

Look and see and we will find
God is kind, yes God is kind.
God is kind to you and me.
We can praise him thankfully.
Look and see and we will find
God is kind, yes God is kind.

2. Go for it!

Have everyone stand in a line in front of you. Chant each line loudly in a military-style rhythm and run-march on the spot.

God is kind, yes God is kind.
God is kind to all mankind.
God is kind in all his ways,
kind to us through all our days.
Watch and learn and keep in mind
that God is kind, yes God is kind.

Discover other people's stories

Choose from the options below to discover people who were (or are) inspired to be kind, like God.

🗣 Tell their story and discuss how they show God's kindness through their actions.

- Boaz and Ruth: Boaz and Ruth showed great kindness. Find the story below.
- David was kind to Jonathan's disabled son. Find the story in your Bible: 2 Samuel 9 or a children's Bible storybook such as *Barnabas Children's Bible*, No. 136.
- Florence Nightingale: a determined woman who showed God's kindness through her nursing abilities. Find her story in *Ten Girls Who Made History* by Irene Howat.
- Tearfund: an organisation bringing help, kindness and relief to people in desperate circumstances across the world. Check out their current programmes and downloadable resources on www.tearfund.org.
- Water Aid: an organisation concerned to bring clean water to the many peoples who still don't have it. The website www.wateraid.org.uk includes a game resource for children.
- Focus on a local hospice for children with life-limiting conditions.

Find Boaz and Ruth's story in Ruth 2; *Barnabas Children's Bible,* No. 104.

Bring: Seven green craft sticks; green playdough

Explain the family relationships, holding up the sticks and telling the story as you draw faces, hair or head coverings at the top of the craft sticks.

Long ago, in biblical times, a woman called Naomi married a man called Elimelech. (*Stick two craft sticks in the playdough to stand them up.*) Naomi and Elimelech had two sons, and life was good. (*Add the two sons.*) But then there came a famine. If there's not enough rain, then crops don't grow well and people can't make bread to eat. Without rain, grass doesn't grow for animals and they die. People run out of food. Naomi and Elimelech and their two sons moved to another country, where there was no famine. (*Move the four craft sticks across the table.*) Even so, after a while, Elimelech died. (*Remove Elimelech.*) Now there were only Naomi and her two sons.

Naomi's sons grew up and married two girls from the new country. (*Add two wives beside the sons.*) But then another sad thing happened. Both Naomi's sons died. (*Remove the two sons.*) Now there were only Naomi and her sons' wives. How awful for them!

Once the famine was over, Naomi decided to go back to her own country. She told the two wives to stay and find new husbands. One of them did just that. (*Remove one of the daughters-in-law.*) But the other one, called Ruth, didn't want to leave Naomi and went with Naomi back to her old country. (*Move the two craft sticks.*)

Everything was strange to Ruth in the new country, but she stayed with Naomi and was kind to her. She picked up leftover grain from the fields so that they could make bread. The man who owned the field was Boaz, and he saw how hard Ruth worked and how kind she was to Naomi. (*Add Boaz beside Ruth.*) Boaz kindly said to Ruth, 'Take as much grain as you need, and there is plenty of water for you to drink.' When Ruth told Naomi what had happened, Naomi asked God to bless Boaz for his kindness, and God did.

 Stick the craft stick characters in your story book.

Consider Boaz and Ruth's story

- How did Ruth show God's kindness?
- How did Boaz show God's kindness?
- I wonder how Naomi felt when heard about Boaz's kindness…
- Ruth showed God's kindness to Naomi, and Boaz showed God's kindness to Naomi and Ruth.

Explore their story

Choose one or more of the activities, depending on your group and time.

1. Growing kindness

Bring: Cress seeds; food trays; kitchen roll

Wet several layers of kitchen roll and lay them in a tray. Gently trace your initials carefully on the paper towels, as large as possible. Carefully scatter cress seeds along the letters.

Say: We are sowing seeds that will grow into cress. We can eat it in salads and sandwiches. *[Name your chosen character]* sowed seeds of kindness that grew, and we can grow seeds of kindness, too.

Children can take home their initialled cress seeds and water them until they have grown.

2. Showing kindness

Bring: Green paper; green paper cake cases; a selection of dried foods, such as popcorn, cereals, dried fruit, pumpkin seeds and potato rings, mixed together in a container

Show the food to the children and see how many different kinds of food they can identify. Fill the paper cake cases with the food for children to enjoy.

Say: There's plenty here for us to share but there are places in the world where the soil isn't good for growing things, or there isn't enough rain to help them grow, or soldiers destroy the crops. How can we show God's kindness to people so far away?

Draw vertical lines from the bottom edge of the sheet of green paper and write ideas along the vertical lines, adding leaves and seeds to make growing plants.

Say: God's kindness is for everyone, and he wants us to share it.

 Stick the picture in your story book.

3. Playtime

Younger children can have a time of free play. If possible, include toys and games that reflect the idea of being kind. For example, bring a pile of socks or gloves and ask children to help sort them into pairs, or peg them to a length of string between two chairs.

♡ Respond

You may like to play a worship CD quietly in the background during this activity.

What about me?

> **Bring:** Apple shapes cut from green paper; pencils

Say: What do you think it means to be kind? Do you know that God wants us to be kind, like him? I would like to be kind like God, and be like *[the character in your chosen story]*. Would you like to be kind? I wonder what we could do that would be kind to people around us…

Listen to the children's ideas, share your own and help them form some practical possibilities, writing them on the apple shapes to take home.

Let's pray

Help children to contribute specific ideas for prayer, using the following pointers. Ask them if there is anything else they would like the group to pray for.

- Let's thank God that he's so kind.
- Sometimes we're not kind like God, and need to tell him that we're sorry.
- Sometimes it's hard to be kind like God, and we need to ask him to help us.

 Record particular prayer requests in your story book.

Review

Look back through your story book. Check where today's Bible stories fit in relation to others already in the book. Look at some previous prayer requests and find out if and how they have been answered. Note any answered prayers in the story book.

Way out

Bring: Green icing; small cakes or cookies

If you made cakes or cookies, you can decorate them and plate them up for the children to offer round the congregation. Alternatively, you can decorate bought biscuits or small cakes.

Take a photograph of either the cakes or cookies you have made, or the congregation enjoying them, and add it to your story book.

Family follow-up

See www.barnabasinchurches.org.uk/extra-resources/ to download the family follow-up sheet.

Play

Find a box with a lid. Decorate it with pictures of food cut from magazines, labels from food products or drawings by the family. Write or draw on slips of green paper ways that God has shown his kindness to the family, and keep them in the box, adding to them as another kindness is shown or remembered.

Invite friends round to retell the story of Jesus feeding the crowd with the boy's lunch. Decide who is playing the different characters and practise the story with simple, exaggerated actions, without speech. You can add music if you wish. Share some food together as part of the story.

Add 'kind' to your 'God is…' collage or patchwork.

Praise

Write out the Bible verse by hand or on a computer and print it out. Stick it on the lid of the box.

Use playdough to fashion the letters KIND and display them where everyone will see them during the week.

The theme colour is green. Using spinach lasagne sheets to make lasagne, adding cooked spinach to the filling and serving with a green salad can act as a reminder to be kind to others, as will playing a game of football on the grass or wearing the colour green for a day.

Plan

Explore one or more of the stories together.

When you're out and about, check on elderly neighbours or relatives who would welcome some kindly help in their home or garden, or with shopping or dog walking. Look for opportunities to be kinder to people whose services we use in shops, call centres, waste collection, postal delivery, school crossing patrols and so on. Share these ideas with the family and encourage each other to acts of kindness.

Ask: What can we do in our family, either together or as individuals, to be kind to each other and to other people? Write, draw or find pictures that represent your ideas and put them in your decorated box. Make plans, dates and times to carry out your ideas. Regularly review how you are doing.

Pray

Thank God for specific things he has kindly given the family. Say sorry to God for particular times when we have forgotten to be kind. Ask for God's help to be kind in specific ways.

*

God is truth

- Theme: Living a truthful life with God
- Learn from Jesus: Luke 19:45–48
- Bible verse: 'Teach me to follow you, and I will obey your truth' (Psalm 86:11a).
- Discover other people's stories: Peter and John; Daniel; John Bunyan; Brother Andrew and Open Doors; Richard Wurmbrand; CARE
- Theme colour: Silver or grey

Way in

What's in the box?

Bring: Silver or grey paper or cloth; magnifying glass; silver chocolate coins in a small box

Cover a table with silver or grey paper or cloth.

Say: I wonder why we are using the colour silver (grey) today...

Put the small box and magnifying glass on the table. Wonder about the objects. Listen and affirm ideas without comment.

Say: I wonder if it's true that the world's tiniest spider is in this box. If it's true, we might need this magnifying glass to see it... We'll open the box later and see if it's true.

Learn from Jesus

Luke 19:45–48: Today's story tells about a time when Jesus got angry with people who weren't truthful. The temple in Jerusalem was a beautiful place where people came to bring their best gifts to God and to worship him.

🎭 Tell the story

Choose the story option most appropriate for your group.

People came to worship God in the temple. They brought their very best lambs for God. (*Stroke the sheet.*) They brought their very best doves for God. (*Flap the sheet.*) They brought their money for God. (*Pick up the sheet to rattle the coins.*) But temple people said, 'Your lamb isn't good enough for God.' (*Stroke the sheet.*) 'Your doves aren't good enough for God.' (*Flap the sheet.*) 'You must buy these better ones instead.' (*Stroke and flap.*) They weren't telling the truth. Their lambs and doves weren't better. (*Stroke and flap.*) They just wanted to make lots of money. (*Rattle the coins.*)

Other temple people said, 'Your money is no good here. You must change it for special temple money.' That wasn't true, either. (*Rattle the coins.*) The temple people kept some of the money for themselves. (*Rattle the coins.*) Jesus watched them. He was very angry with the temple people for telling lies and cheating. He said, 'You've made God's house a place where robbers hide!' He tipped over their tables and stalls. Everything flapped, rolled, ran and baa-ed all over the place. What a mess! What a noise! (*Shake the sheet and let the money roll.*)

1. Money! Money! Money!

Bring: A white sheet; 5p, 10p, 20p and 50p coins or silver play coins

Put the coins on the spread-out sheet. Sit around the sheet. Tell the story, pausing to all do the actions.

2. Sound it out!

Read the story, setting the scene. Instead of actions, make up sound effects as an accompaniment to the story. Listen to children's ideas before suggesting any of the following.

- **Temple traders:** Market shouts, such as 'Three for the price of two!' 'Buy one, get one free!' 'Best rates for money changing!'
- **Lambs:** Baa-aa
- **Doves:** Coo
- **Money:** Chink-a-chink

Read the story again, pausing for sound effects.

3. Find the story in the Bible

An adult or child may read Luke 19:45–48 from a Bible or children's Bible storybook such *Barnabas Children's Bible*, No. 297.

Consider the story

- I wonder how people felt when they were told that their lambs and doves weren't good enough for God…
- I wonder what the temple people did when Jesus tipped over their tables…
- What did we find out about Jesus in that story?
- Jesus loves the truth. God is truth.

 Explore the story

Choose one or more of the activities, depending on your group and time.

1. Find the coins!

Bring: Grey or silver wax crayons

Using the coins from the story, cover them with paper and use the wax crayons to make rubbings.

Stick coin rubbings in your story book.

2. Foreign exchange

Bring: Foreign currency; world map

Identify the currencies and the countries they come from, then find the countries on the map. Explain that we have to use the coins and notes of the country we visit. We must change our money into theirs while we are there.

Say: In our Bible story, the temple traders used different coins from the rest of the country. Ordinary people couldn't spend their own money at the temple. They had to change it for temple coins. The temple traders cheated people as they changed their money, and lied about how much their coins were worth.

3. Tell the truth!

Say: I'm going to tell you one true thing about me and one thing that isn't true. You can guess which thing is the truth.

Briefly tell one truth and one falsehood. Give others the opportunity to do the same for everyone to guess.

Say: It's not always easy to tell when people are telling the truth. It's always easy to tell when God is telling the truth, because he *always* tells the truth. Amazing!

⊙ Time to praise God

Hold up a Bible. Explain that the Bible story told us that Jesus hates lies and loves the truth. Jesus shows us what God is like. God is truth.

It tells us in the Bible

Teach me to follow you, and I will obey your truth. (Psalm 86:11a)

Bring: Grey paper

Draw round shoes on the grey paper and cut them out. Lay the footsteps in a winding path. Walk along the path, stepping on the footsteps and saying the verse aloud. Have everyone follow in turn.

Stick a pair of footsteps, with the verse written across them, in your story book.

Music praise

You can sing together or along with a CD or DVD. Some children may prefer to do actions, dance or jump around rather than sing. Alternatively, you can play a CD while doing the Bible verse activity. Choose songs relating to God's truthfulness (see page 19 for suggested CDs).

Activity options

1. Singing rhyme

Move the paper footsteps to form a circle and walk round them while singing the rhyme below, to the tune 'The wheels on the bus'.

Let's make a circle while we will sing,
while we will sing, while we will sing.
Let's make a circle while we will sing,
all day long.

And God will teach us his best ways,
his best ways, his best ways.
And God will teach us his best ways,
all day long.

And in God's truth we all can walk,
we all can walk, we all can walk.
And in God's truth we all can walk,
all day long.

2. Scents of praise

Bring: Air freshener or candle, scented with incense or spices

Say: The temple was a beautiful place, full of colour, light and inviting smells. It wasn't a quiet place. It was full of people celebrating God. There was singing and instruments of all kinds. There were shouts of praise to God, too. People enjoyed celebrating God. Let's make some shouts of praise to God. What words can we use?

Help children formulate a few sentences, such as, 'I will praise you, Lord, with all my heart'; 'Praise you, Lord, for you are good'; 'We worship you in the beauty of your temple.'

Safely light the candle or activate the air freshener. Shout your praises together. You can also play loud music if you wish.

Discover other people's stories

Choose from the options below to discover people who endeavoured to be truthful, like God.

Tell their story and discuss how they show God's truthfulness through their actions

- Peter and John told the truth that Jesus had risen from death. Find the story below.
- Daniel told the truth to Belshazzar. Find the story in your Bible: Daniel 5 or a children's Bible storybook such as *Barnabas Children's Bible*, No. 219.
- John Bunyan was imprisoned for teaching, preaching and writing the truth. Find the story in *Ten Boys Who Used their Talents* by Irene Howat.
- Brother Andrew carried God's truth behind the Iron Curtain and founded Open Doors (see www.opendoorsuk.org).
- Richard Wurmbrand was imprisoned for preaching the truth. Find his story on Torchlighters *Heroes of the Faith* DVD.
- CARE communicates God's truth through family support, research, guidance and parliamentary campaigning (see www.care.org.uk).
- Focus on a local person, organisation or charity exhibiting God's truthfulness.

Find Peter and John's story in Acts 4:1–22; *Barnabas Children's Bible*, No. 321.

Make a simple prison with a circle of chairs. Sit inside as prisoners alongside Peter and John. Pause to check the prisoners' reactions at different points in the story.

Peter and John showed a beggar God's goodness at the temple, and healed him in the name of Jesus. After that, everyone wanted to hear what Peter and John said about Jesus. Peter and John told the truth that Jesus had been killed but was alive again, raised by God's power. The priests and elders at the temple were angry with Peter and John for talking about Jesus in this way. They had Peter and John arrested and put in prison.

Prisoners, if you ask Peter and John why they are in prison, what will they say? What do you think about them being in prison with you?

The next morning, the high priest and other elders asked Peter and John how the crippled man had been healed. The Holy Spirit helped Peter to tell the truth, that the power of Jesus had healed him. This was the same Jesus whom they had put to death on a cross and God had raised to life. That was the same Jesus who had come to save people from their sins. The high priest and elders didn't want to believe Peter but they had no reason to keep Peter and John in prison. They had to let them go, but told them not to talk about Jesus any more. Peter was truthful and said they couldn't agree to that. They would carry on telling that truth that Jesus was alive—and they did.

And what about you prisoners? Having been with Peter and John and heard what they said, what do you think about Jesus now?

Consider Peter and John's story

- What did we find out about Peter and John in that story?
- I wonder what happened when Peter and John carried on telling the truth about Jesus…
- Peter and John were truthful, like God.

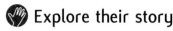 Explore their story

Choose one or more of the activities, depending on your group and time.

1. Truth poster

> **Bring:** Grey paper with 'truth' written in large, outline letters; silver paper or tinfoil

Tear the paper and foil into small pieces and stick them to the letters.

Say: If *[name your chosen character]* had kept quiet about Jesus or not told the truth, their life might have been easier. The Holy Spirit helped them and they chose to tell the truth. God's truth will always shine out.

 Stick the poster in your story book.

2. Tell the truth!

> **Bring:** A pack of drinking straws

Hold the stack of straws upright, then let them go on a table. Everyone can take turns to try to pick up straws without making any others move. Different colours can be given different values, to be added up at the end.

Say: When it's our turn and we make other straws move, we don't always want to tell the truth. God wants us always to be truthful.

3. Playtime

Younger children can have a time of free play. If possible, include toys and puzzles that require children to be truthful—for example, memory games.

 Respond

You may like to play a worship CD quietly in the background during this activity.

What about me?

Bring: Tinfoil squares; smaller grey paper squares

Say: What do you think it means to be truthful? Do you know that God wants us to be truthful, like him? I would like to be truthful, like God, and like *[the character in your chosen story]*. Would you like to be truthful? I wonder what we could do that would help us tell the truth…

Listen to the children's ideas, share your own and help them form some practical possibilities. Help children to write their ideas on the grey squares and stick them on the tinfoil squares to take home. If you used the coin rubbing activity, your rubbings could be cut into squares and used instead.

Let's pray

Help children to contribute specific ideas for prayer, using the following pointers. Ask them if there is anything else they would like the group to pray for.

- Let's thank God that he is truth.
- Sometimes we lie, and need to tell God that we're sorry.
- Sometimes it's hard to be truthful like God, and we need to ask him to help us.

 Record particular prayer requests in your story book.

Review

Look back through your story book. Check where today's Bible stories fit in relation to others already in the book. Look at some previous prayer requests and find out if and how they have been answered. Note any answered prayers in the story book.

Way out

Show the box and magnifying glass from the beginning of the session.

Say: I wonder if it's true that the world's tiniest spider is in this box... If so, we might need the magnifying glass to see it...

Ask someone to open the box. Someone else can use the magnifying glass.

Say: It's true that some creatures God has made are so tiny that they can't be seen without a magnifying glass, but none of them are in this box—and that's the truth.

Share the silver chocolate coins.

Family follow-up

See www.barnabasinchurches.org.uk/extra-resources/ to download the family follow-up sheet.

Play

Games such as 'battleships', 'pick up sticks', memory games and so on give opportunities to choose truthfulness or lying. Consider God's perspective and develop strategies to deal with the unfairness that lying causes when it happens.

As you watch TV or films or sports together, look out for people telling the truth or lying and cheating. Talk about their reasons for doing so, and the consequences.

Add 'truth' to your 'God is...' collage or patchwork.

Praise

Walk up the stairs, saying one word of the Bible verse and reference on each stair. If you have no stairs, march together on the spot.

Use magnetic letters to write the word 'truth' on the fridge as a family reminder that God is all truth, and wants us to be truthful.

The theme colour is silver or grey. Look for silvery snail or slug trails on paths and pavements. Everywhere they go, they leave a slimy, silvery trail. When we don't tell the truth, we leave a trail, too, slimy and slippery for others to get caught up in. Better to be truthful, and leave no trail. Use grey, cloudy days or sparkling silver frost as a reminder to be more truthful.

Plan

Explore one or more of the stories together.

When you're out and about look for opportunities to be truthful and that moment of decision before telling the truth, or not. Share the challenges with the rest of the family.

Ask: What can we do in our family, either together or as individuals, to live a truthful life with God? At family meal times, encourage each other to tell truthfully of successes and failures.

Pray

Thank God that he is truth, unchanging. Say sorry to God for particular times when we have been untruthful. Ask for God's help to be more truthful.

✳

God is gentle

- **Theme:** Showing God's gentleness
- **Learn from Jesus:** Luke 7:11–17
- **Bible verse:** 'Learn from me, for I am gentle and humble in heart' (Matthew 11:29, NIV).
- **Discover other people's stories:** Mary; Elijah; Cicily Saunders; Mary Slessor; Halo Trust
- **Theme colour:** Pink

Way in

Yummy pink!

> **Bring:** Pink paper or cloth; box of pink tissues; pack of pink and white marshmallows

Cover a table with pink paper or cloth.

Say: I wonder why we are using the colour pink today…

Put the tissues and marshmallows on the table. Listen and affirm ideas without comment. Share out some marshmallows and save the rest for later.

Ask: Which of these words describes marshmallows best: crunchy, hard, gentle, salty, chewy?

If you have boys who are put off by the colour pink, explain that until recent times pink was thought of a strong, manly colour, because it's light red and any kind of red was a forceful colour. Blue was always thought of as a girl's colour.

Learn from Jesus

Luke 7:11–17: Today's story tells about a time when Jesus showed God's gentleness to someone who was hurting badly. The town of Nain had a wall around it, with gates for people and animals to pass through. At night, the gates were shut to keep out robbers and enemies, and no one could go in or out. Jesus and his friends came to Nain and were just about to go in through the gate when they had to stop to let a crowd of people squeeze out from inside the town.

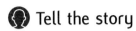 Tell the story

Choose the story option most appropriate for your group.

Jesus and his friends have walked a long way. There's Jesus and Peter and Andrew and John and Thomas and Nathaniel and all the others. Can you see how tired and dusty they all look after their long walk?

Jesus and his friends see the high stone wall around the town of Nain. Can you see that high, solid wall?

Jesus and his friends see the open gateway and the strong gate with wooden bars ready to put across it at night. Can you see the gateway and the gate?

Then Jesus and his friends hear lots of people from inside the town, crying, wailing and shouting. Can you hear them? Whatever can be the matter?

Clouds of dust and a crush of people are squeezing and squashing through the gate. Can you see them almost falling over each other?

Some men carry a stretcher between them. There are so many people pressed together. Can you see the stretcher almost tipping over in the crowd?

A woman is hanging on to the stretcher. She's crying hard and can't see where she's going. Can you see her, poor woman? I wonder why she's so upset. She needs more than one tissue.

Jesus makes a way through the people to get to the woman. Watch him. Go, Jesus!

Jesus sees a dead boy lying on the stretcher. Can you see him, lying so still?

The woman's husband had died. Now her boy is dead, too. How does Jesus look?

Jesus says, 'Don't cry'. He touches the stretcher. The men carrying it stop. Can you see them, waiting, trying to hold the stretcher still?

Jesus speaks to the dead boy and tells him to get up. The boy sits up, alive again, and begins to talk. Can you see him, sitting there, talking?

Jesus gives the boy to his mother. What is she doing? Can you see her laughing, crying and hugging him? What are the crowd doing?

1. I can see it!

Give everyone a pink tissue and ask them to close their eyes.

Say: I am going to draw a picture for you to see inside your head. Ready? Then read the story.

2. Sounds of life

Tell the children that this is a sad story with a happy ending. Make up and practise some sad sounds and happy sounds.

Read the story without the mind pictures. Signal the sad sounds to begin before the people start coming through the gate. Signal the change to sad and happy sounds together when Jesus goes to the mother. Signal the change to all happy sounds when the boy is healed and the people are amazed and full of joy.

3. Find the story in the Bible

An adult or child may read Luke 7:11–17 from a Bible or children's Bible storybook such as *Barnabas Children's Bible*, No. 267.

Consider the story

- I wonder how Jesus felt when he saw the boy's mother…
- I wonder what the boy said when he sat up on the stretcher…
- What did we find out about Jesus in that story?
- Jesus is gentle, like God.

🖐 Explore the story

Choose one or more of the activities, depending on your group and time.

1. Gentle heart

Bring: Pink crêpe paper hearts, about 12cm high (two per person); tissues; pink wool; stapler

Staple two hearts together, leaving the top open. Stuff with tissues. Staple the top of the heart, adding a loop of wool for hanging at home.

Say: This is to remind you that Jesus is gentle.

2. God's heart

Bring: Pink card; pink wool; scissors; sticky tape; hole punch

Cut out a heart shape. Punch holes around the edge. Cut a length of wool and tape the end to make a 'needle'. Weave the wool in and out of the holes. Tie a loop of wool to the top of the heart for hanging at home.

Say: The heart is a strong muscle, working hard all the time. The gentleness Jesus showed came from God's heart of love, strong and working to heal.

 Stick a heart shape in your story book.

3. Hold on!

Partner everyone as evenly as possible. Partners stand facing each other, holding each other's forearms. One partner gently stands on the other's feet, still holding on. Now they can try to walk. At each step, the bottom feet must lift off the ground and the top feet keep touching the ones underneath.

Say: We don't want to hurt each other, so we put our feet down firmly but gently. We need to be strong and hold on. Gentleness can be strong.

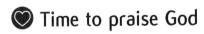 Time to praise God

Hold up a Bible. Explain that the Bible story told us that Jesus is gentle. Jesus shows us what God is like.

It tells us in the Bible

'Learn from me, for I am gentle and humble in heart.' (Matthew 11:29)

Say the verse aloud.

Say: I wonder what 'humble' means… 'Humble' means not making yourself out to be big and important. More than anyone, Jesus has the right to be big and important because Jesus is the Son of God. But Jesus was gentle and humble, and he wants us to be like him.

Repeat the verse several times with the following actions.

* Learn: Open book with hands
* From me: Point to self
* For I am gentle: Hug self
* And humble: Hold out hands
* In heart: Clench a fist and pulse it on your heart

Music praise

You can sing together or along with a CD or DVD. Some children may prefer to do actions, dance or jump around rather than sing. Alternatively you can play a CD while doing the Bible verse activity. Choose songs relating to God's gentleness (see page 19 for suggested CDs).

Activity options

1. Gentle waves!

Bring: Pink crêpe paper streamers

Sing the rhyme to the tune 'London Bridge is falling down'. Add the actions with the streamers.

Jesus! Jesus! Gentle, strong (Wave streamers)
Gentle, strong, gentle, strong (Clench a fist and pulse it on your heart)
Jesus! Jesus! Gentle, strong (Wave streamers)
Jesus! Jesus! (Clench a fist and pulse it on your heart)

2. Rhythm rap

Read the rap below loudly in rhythm and encourage children to experiment with energetic moves and break dance.

Take your fingers out your ears and listen up to me.
Listen, now! Listen! That's the way it's gonna be!
God puts his gentleness in every human frame,
To care, to give, to bless, to heal, all in his holy name.
Are you ready now you people, to come along with me?
We'll do some moves together as we solve this mystery.
God wants you to play your part, with gentleness in your heart.
Gentleness, the strongest act. Mystery? Yes! Ain't that a fact!

Discover other people's stories

Choose from the options below to discover people who were (or are) inspired to be gentle, like God.

Tell their story and discuss how they show God's gentleness through their actions.

- Mary gently washed Jesus' feet with her hair. Find the story below.
- Elijah gently healed and restored the widow's son. Find the story in your Bible: 1 Kings 17:17–24 or a children's Bible storybook such as *Barnabas Children's Bible*, No. 164.
- Cicely Saunders: founder of the modern hospice movement (see www.stchristophers.org.uk).
- Mary Slessor: Scottish missionary to Nigeria. Find her story in *Ten Girls Who Changed the World* by Irene Howat or see www.maryslessor.org.
- Halo Trust: clearing minefields needs gentleness and a steady hand. It also needs great courage, determination and a strong mind (see www.halotrust.org).
- Focus on a local person, organisation or charity that exhibits and spreads God's gentleness.

Find Mary's story in John 12:1–8; *Barnabas Children's Bible,* No. 295.

Bring: Air freshener or candle with a fragrance such as sandalwood or cedarwood; matches

Sit in a circle. Place the air freshener or lit candle safely in the centre. Those who wish to do so can remove their shoes and socks. All join in the actions.

Jesus lived in a hot and dusty country. When you went to someone's house, they took off your sandals and washed and dried your dusty feet. Ahh! There's nothing like having your feet washed for you, and being fresh and clean. *(Wiggle toes.)*

Jesus went to visit his friends Lazarus, Martha and Mary. They always made him very welcome and looked after him and his friends. Mary came to wash Jesus' feet. *(Wiggle toes.)* But instead of bringing a bowl of water and a towel as usual, she poured some very expensive perfume over Jesus' feet and gently wiped them with her hair. *(Breathe deeply.)* The perfume filled the whole house. *(Breathe deeply.)*

Another of Jesus' friends, Judas, said, 'What a waste of money!' *(Wiggle toes.)* Judas said, 'That money could have been used to help people in need.' But Mary had given Jesus the very best because she loved him. *(Breathe deeply.)* Judas was not to be trusted. He looked after the money for Jesus and his friends, and often stole it for himself. Jesus knew all about Judas.

Jesus knew all about Mary, too, and knew that she had done this costly, gentle thing for him. *(Breathe deeply.)* Jesus told Judas to leave Mary alone. Jesus knew that soon he would have to leave his friends and go alone to die. Mary's gentleness helped Jesus to be strong to face what lay ahead. *(Breathe deeply.)*

Blow out the candle and remove it safely.

Consider Mary's story

- What did we find out about Mary in that story?
- I wonder how long the perfume lasted in the house, on Mary's hair and on Jesus' feet…
- Mary was gentle, like God.

 Everyone can pull one hair out of their scalp. Stick the hairs to a sheet of pink paper and, when the candle has cooled, rub the candle across the paper to transfer its scent. Stick the paper in your story book.

Explore their story

Choose one or more activity, depending on your group and time.

1. I can do that!

Bring: An old telephone directory

Tear out one sheet for each person from the directory. Waft the pages up and down.

Say: I can create a gentle breeze with this page. It's thin paper.

Tear your sheet in half.

Say: And it's not very strong.

Take the whole directory and try to tear it in half. Offer it to others who would like to try.

Say: The telephone directory is made up of all these gentle, not very strong pages, but it's very strong indeed. Gentle can be strong. *[Name your chosen character]* was gentle but strong and determined. Jesus was gentle but very, very strong.

2. Portrait

Bring: Card; paints; mixing trays; large potatoes; knife; drinking straws

Cut potatoes in half.

Say: What do you think *[name your chosen character]* might have looked like? Was she young, elderly or in between? What colour were her eyes... and her hair?

The ideas suggested don't have to be the same. Mix paints to match a skin tone. Dip the cut side of a potato in the paint and press on to the card. Mix runny paint to make your chosen hair colours and pour a little around each head. With a straw, blow the hair paint gently to the right length and style. When the face is dry, features can be added.

Say: *[Name character]* was gentle but strong and determined.

 Stick a named portrait in your story book.

3. Playtime

Younger children can have a time of free play. If possible, include toys and games that relate to gentleness, such as blowing bubbles or keeping balloons up in the air.

Respond

You may like to play a worship CD quietly in the background during this activity.

What about me?

> **Bring:** Pink fluorescent pens

Say: What do you think it means to be gentle? Do you know that God wants us to be gentle, like him? I would like to be gentle like God, and be like *[the character in your chosen story]*. Would you like to be gentle? I wonder what we could do that would be gentle...

Listen to the children's ideas, share your own and help them form some practical possibilities. Write them on the torn pieces of telephone directory with the pink fluorescent pens, for the children to take home.

Let's pray

Help children to contribute specific ideas for prayer, using the following pointers. Ask them if there is anything else they would like the group to pray for.

- Let's thank God that he's so gentle.
- Sometimes we're not gentle like God, and we can tell him that we're sorry.
- Sometimes it's hard to be gentle like God, and we need to ask him to help us.

 Record particular prayer requests in your story book.

Review

Look back through your story book. Check where today's Bible stories fit in relation to others already in the book. Look at some previous prayer requests and find out if and how they have been answered. Note any answered prayers in the story book.

Way out

Share out the remainder of the marshmallows. Holding a marshmallow in the hand, have everyone say, 'Gentle and strong' several times quickly before eating the marshmallows.

Family follow-up

See www.barnabasinchurches.org.uk/extra-resources/ to download the family follow-up sheet.

Play

Have a tug of war to test the gentle strength of rolls of good-quality kitchen paper.

Make cupcakes with pink icing. Before any food colouring is added, separate the icing into four small bowls. Add varying drops of colour to create shades from almost red to the barest hint of pink.

If you have a buzz wire game, play it together. We have to be gentle and keep a very steady hand to play this game.

Add 'gentle' to your 'God is…' collage or patchwork.

Praise

Using thin pink card, bubble-write either all the individual letters or the words of the Bible verse and cut them out. Muddle them up and then put the words in order. Muddle them up again for someone else to have a turn later.

The theme colour is pink. Making a salad dressing with tomato ketchup and mayonnaise mixed together, slowly and gently eating pomegranate seeds together with cocktail sticks, or looking out for pink-ribbed tomato seeds to grow, are all great reminders of God's gentleness.

Plan

Explore one or more of the stories together.

When you're out and about, look for examples of people being gentle to others, such as a busy mother with small children or a young person gently respecting someone elderly. Share good and bad examples with the family.

Ask: Who do we learn our patterns of speech, our attitudes and actions from? Who are we influenced by? Is it Jesus? Is home the first or last place where gentleness is exhibited? What can we do in our family, either together or as individuals, to show God's gentleness?'

Pray

Thank God for any specific ways in which he has shown gentleness to the family. Say sorry to God for any particular times when we have not shown his gentleness to others. Ask for God's help to be gentle in the ways we have identified.

*

God is joyful

- **Theme:** Sharing God's joy
- **Learn from Jesus:** Luke 15:1–7
- **Bible verse:** 'The Lord your God is with you, he is mighty to save. He will take great delight in you, he will quiet you with his love, he will rejoice over you with singing' (Zephaniah 3:17, NIV).
- **Discover other people's stories:** Moses and Miriam; angels; Big Ministries; Ishmael; Johann Sebastian Bach
- **Theme colour:** White

Way in

Joyful bubbles!

Bring: White paper or cloth; pots of bubbles or a bubble-making machine

Cover a table with white paper or cloth.

Say: I wonder why we are using the colour white today…

Put the pots of bubbles on the table.

Say: I wonder what the word 'joy' means…

Listen and affirm ideas without comment. Blow bubbles or have the machine blow them out continuously. Everyone can join in the refrain as you chant.

Joy is not just happy.
It's a whole lot more than that!
Joy is not just cheerful.
It's a whole lot more than that!
Joy is not just glad.
It's a whole lot more than that!
Joy is not just jolly.
It's a whole lot more than that!
Joy is bigger than all of those.
It's a whole lot bigger than all of those!

Learn from Jesus

Luke 15:1–7: In today's story, Jesus tells people how much joy God feels about everyone. People loved to listen to Jesus and he often told them stories to help them understand about God. Jesus told this story to show how God is filled with joy for the people he loves.

🎭 Tell the story

Choose the story option most appropriate for your group.

A shepherd had one hundred sheep. Every day he counted them to make sure none had got lost.

Counting sheep is hard because they don't stand still. 97, 98, 99… Stand still, sheep! The shepherd counted them again. 97, 98, 99… Stand still, sheep! He counted them again. 97, 98, 99… Definitely, one sheep was missing. The shepherd went to look for the one lost sheep.

At last, the shepherd found it. The shepherd carried the sheep home on his shoulder. The sheep joined all the others again. The shepherd was more than happy—he was full of joy. He told his friends, 'Come and share my joy, because I found my lost sheep.'

Jesus said that we're like that lost sheep. We get lost in doing wrong things and, when God finds us, he's full of joy. Heaven has a big party!

1. There's always one!

> **Bring:** The fingers cut from old pairs of gloves; PVA glue; plate; small pieces of cotton wool

Put a glove finger on an index finger, roll it into the glue and then cover it in cotton wool. Make several woolly sheep in the same way. Everyone can wiggle their sheep as you tell the story. Keep one of your own sheep out of sight until the lost sheep is found.

 Put a sheep into a polythene pocket and place in your story book.

2. Full of joy!

Bring: A sheepskin rug

Tell the story.

Say: Sheep are not very clever animals and find it easy to get into trouble. There were rocky places where sheep could fall down, fiercely sharp thorn bushes to get stuck in, and predators looking for a sheep-shaped meal.

In turn, children can put the sheepskin over a shoulder, pretending to be the lost sheep, and answer questions, such as the following examples.

- Why did you wander off from the rest of the flock?
- What happened to you?
- Were you frightened?
- How long were you out there on your own?
- Did you think the shepherd wouldn't bother coming back?
- How did you feel when the shepherd found you?

Say: Jesus said we are like that lost sheep. When we are found, God is full, full, full of joy.

3. Find the story in the Bible

An adult or child may read Luke 15:1–7 from a Bible or children's Bible storybook such as *Barnabas Children's Bible*, No. 281.

Consider the story

- I wonder why Jesus told that story…
- What did we find out about God in that story?
- God is full of joy.

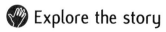 Explore the story

Choose one or more of the activities, depending on your group and time.

1. Flags of joy

Bring: Short garden canes; squares of fabric; fabric paints

Paint the word 'JOY' on the fabric and decorate around the letters. Fix the fabric to a garden cane with sticky tape to make a flag.

2. Joy uncontained!

Bring: Washing-up liquid; powder paint; containers; drinking straws; garden canes

Pour a quarter of a cup of washing-up liquid into a container. Mix a small amount of water with the powder paint and add to the washing-up liquid to make a bright colour. Gently blow (not suck!) the paint mixture until the bubbles overflow the container. Roll paper around gently on top of the bubbles without pressing and bursting the bubbles. To make multicoloured bubbles, more than one colour can be used on each sheet.

When dry, the sheets can be fixed to garden canes with sticky tape to make a flag.

3. Bubbling up!

Bring: A pot of bubbles; fizzy drink or sherbet sweets; bubblewrap; camera

Say: I wonder what it feels like to be full of joy…

Listen to children's ideas.

Say: Sometimes joy might bubble up, gently and unexpectedly. *(Blow bubbles over everyone.)*

Sometimes joy might fizz, fast and dizzy. *(Children can try the fizzy drink or sherbet.)*

Sometimes joy might explode like fireworks on Bonfire Night. *(Jump on the bubble wrap.)*

Sometimes joy just can't keep still. Let's move it! *(Dance, jump, clap widely and so on.)*

Say: God is full of joy for us! And God wants us to share his joy!

Take some photographs for your story book.

Time to praise God

Hold up a Bible. Explain that the Bible story told us that God is full of joy for us. Jesus shows us what God is like.

It tells us in the Bible

The Lord your God is with you, he is mighty to save. He will take great delight in you, he will quiet you with his love, he will rejoice over you with singing. (Zephaniah 3:17, NIV)

> **Bring:** A white long-sleeved jumper; six white postcards; white wool; hole punch

Write out each phrase of the verse and the reference, one on each card. Punch a hole in the two top corners of the cards. Thread wool through each one, and tie, making a loop. A volunteer can put on the white jumper and hold out their arms at the sides. Everyone else can hang the looped cards over the arms of the person wearing the jumper.

Pointing to the cards in order, read the whole verse together.

Music praise

You can sing together or along with a CD or DVD. Some children may prefer to do actions, dance or jump around rather than sing. Alternatively, you can play a CD while doing the Bible verse activity. Choose songs relating to God's joy (see page 19 for suggested CDs).

Activity options

1. Flags of joy

Wave the flags your made earlier, while dancing and chanting the following lines.

God is full of joy, God is full of joy.
We can dance, we can sing, God is full of joy.

2. Ha ha!

Three or four people can do this activity together. If there are more people in your group, split into twos or threes. Sit close together and look at each other. The first person says, 'Ha'; the next person says, 'Ha'; the next person says, 'Ha', and so on. Gradually increase the speed until someone breaks out into laughter.
Say: God is full of joy over us, bubbling up and breaking out.

Discover other people's stories

Choose from the options below to discover people who were (or are) inspired to share God's joy.

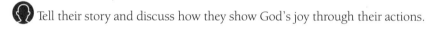 Tell their story and discuss how they show God's joy through their actions.

- Moses and Miriam praised God for his deliverance with great joy. Find the story below.
- Angels brought news of great joy to the shepherds. Find the story in your Bible: Luke 2:8–20 or a children's Bible storybook such as *Barnabas Children's Bible*, No. 248.
- Johann Sebastian Bach: through good times and bad, he found God's joy in music. Find his story in *Ten Boys Who Used their Talents* by Irene Howat.
- Big Ministries, Ishmael or other people travelling around churches, teaching and partying with God's joy. See www.bigministries.co.uk and www.ishmael. org.uk.
- Focus on a local person, organisation or charity that shares and spreads God's joy.

Find Moses and Miriam's story in Exodus 15:1–2, 19–21; *Barnabas Children's Bible*, No. 51

> **Bring:** Musical instruments

Give out instruments and have everyone play them at the beginning of the story, so quietly that they can hardly be heard. As you tell the story expressively, gradually increase the sound until, at the end of the story, you are shouting God's praise.

The great and mighty Pharaoh sent 600 speedy chariots, plus foot soldiers and horses, to catch up with Moses and God's people out in the desert. He had set them free but then changed his mind and wanted them back as his slaves.

But God, so much greater than Pharaoh and almighty in power, made a way through the sea for all his people to safely cross it. When the soldiers followed close behind, God closed up the sea again and all the soldiers were swept away. When God's people were all safely on the shore and saw what God had done, they were filled with such joy that they could hardly contain it.

Moses sang a wonderful song of praise to God. Miriam, his sister, led the women in a dance and they played their tambourines for God, sharing his joy together. How great is our God! And full of joy for us!

Sing or play the chorus from the song 'How great is our God' by Chris Tomlin. Join in, wave flags, play instruments or dance around.

Consider Moses and Miriam's story

- What did we find out about Moses and Miriam in that story?
- I wonder how we might have felt if our families were being chased by Egyptian soldiers…
- The Bible tells us that Moses trusted God.
- Moses and Miriam were full of joy, like God.

🖐 Explore their story

Choose one or more of the activities, depending on your group and time.

1. Explosions of joy!

> **Bring:** A play parachute or piece of fabric appropriate for your group size; small plastic lightweight balls

Give everyone several balls and sit around the parachute. Ask questions about your chosen story. As children contribute answers, they can throw the balls on to the parachute. Questions might include the following.

- God's people had been slaves for a long, long time. How did they feel when at last Pharaoh agreed to let them go?
- How did they feel when Pharaoh changed his mind and sent soldiers to take them back to Egypt?
- What did people say when they reached the sea and found that there was no way forward and no way back?
- When God opened up a path through the sea, what did they think?
- When everyone was safe and the sea rolled back over the soldiers, what did they think then?

Say: 'Joy' is such a little word for a big feeling.
   Stand up and have everyone grasp the parachute.
   Say: God's joy can explode from people!
   Toss the parachute up and down until all the balls have bounced off.

2. A life of joy!

> **Bring:** A large sheet of paper

Divide the paper into seven sections and make a horizontal line halfway down. Talk about Moses, the shepherds, Bach or a Christian who has died that the children knew. Take turns to draw the pictures.

1. *(Point to the first blank space above the horizontal line.)* Long before Moses was even born, God planned him and looked forward to him with great joy.
2. *(Draw a stick baby, with legs and arms in the air.)* God was full of joy when Moses was born.
3. *(Draw a stick baby with arms and legs on the floor, trying to stand.)* When Moses first stood up, God was full of joy.
4. *(Draw a standing child.)* When Moses was a child, God was full of joy for him.
5. *(Draw an adult stick figure.)* When Moses grew up, God was still full of joy for him.
6. *(Draw a slightly bent stick figure.)* When Moses grew old, God was still full of joy for him.
7. *(Point to the blank space.)* When Moses went back to be with God, can you imagine God's joy, and Moses'?

3. Playtime

Younger children can have a time of free play. If possible, include toys and games that relate to joy. Provide old magazines for children to tear up and stuff into carrier bags. When full, tie the tops of the bags and children can then toss or kick them around.

 Respond

You may like to play a worship CD quietly in the background during this activity.

What about me?

Say: What do you think it means to be full of joy? Do you know that God wants to share his joy with us? I would like to share God's joy and be like *[the character in your chosen story]*. Would you like to share God's joy? I wonder how we could show God's joy…

Listen to children's ideas, share your own and help them form some possibilities. Help children to write their ideas on the back of their flags to take home.

Let's pray

Help children to contribute specific ideas for prayer, using the following pointers. Ask if there is anything else they would like the group to pray for.

- Let's thank God that he is full of joy.
- When we do wrong, we can be truly sorry and know the joy of God's forgiveness.
- We can ask God to share his joy with us.

 Record particular prayer requests in your story book.

Review

Look back through your story book. Check where today's Bible stories fit in relation to others already in the book. Look at some previous prayer requests and find out if and how they have been answered. Note any answered prayers in the story book.

Way out

Say: Close your eyes. I'm going to blow some bubbles towards you. As they flutter on your face, remember that God wants to share his joy with you.

Family follow-up

See www.barnabasinchurches.org.uk/extra-resources/ to download the family follow-up sheet.

Play

Make your own bubble mix or buy pots. Whose bubbles can float the highest? Who can blow the biggest bubble? Who can make the most bubbles in one minute? Alternatively, use drinking straws in a bubble bath to blow up a bubble storm.

Make popcorn and enjoy the explosion of joy. Watch the funniest DVD you can find and eat the popcorn together.

Add 'joyful' to your 'God is…' collage or patchwork.

Praise

Make a mobile of the Bible verse. Using white paper, draw six wide spirals. Write the six sections of the verse on them, then cut out the spirals. Cover a wire coat hanger with white tissues. Use white thread and a hole punch to hang the six parts of the verse at varying heights. Hang the mobile where everyone can see it, and read the verse aloud at bedtime.

Use magnetic letters to spell out 'joy' on the fridge. Smile every time you open the fridge.

The theme colour is white. Finding a field of sheep to watch, looking out for sheep trials in your area, making the best mashed potato with grated white Cheshire cheese or being the first to shout, 'Joy!' whenever you see a white van on the road will all help to remind everyone that God is joyful.

Plan

Explore one or more of the stories together.

When you're out and about, look for people sharing joyful times together. Share these with the rest of the family.

Ask: What can we do as a family, either together or as individuals, to be more aware of God's joy and to share in it? Encourage everyone to find a quiet place for a few minutes, just to sit and wonder about God's joy in you. Try to imagine God singing over you with great delight and joy. How would that sound? Make space to share what everyone thought.

Pray

Thank God for his amazing and constant joy over each family member. Name each person in turn, asking God to bless them with his joy. Ask God to help you be more aware of his joy in yourselves, and in each other.

Side by Side with God in Everyday Life

Helping children to grow with God through all times

Yvonne Morris

Side by Side with God in Everyday Life invites churches and families alike to use a simple retelling of stories from the Bible as the basis for helping children to think more deeply about a wide range of everyday topics.

In total there are 28 easy-to-use story-based sessions, each featuring one of the times and seasons outlined in Ecclesiastes 3:1–8, such as birth, death, planting, uprooting, laughing, mourning, dancing, giving, listening, love, hate, war and peace.

Each session picks out two related Bible stories, one to set the scene and the other to go deeper into the theme. The idea is that these simple retellings can be used to promote open questions, reflection, discussion, further exploration and prayer, and readily act as prompts towards a deeper understanding of what it means to walk side by side with God in everything we do.

ISBN 978 1 84101 855 3   £7.99

Available from your local Christian bookshop or, in case of difficulty, direct from BRF: please visit www.barnabasinchurches.org.uk.

Through the Year with Jesus!

A once-a-month children's programme for small churches

Eleanor Zuercher

Following the success of *Not Sunday, Not School!*, Eleanor Zuercher has developed an exciting further year's worth of themed material, based on aspects of the life and teaching of Jesus.

The material is explored through a wealth of creative and interactive activities and, as before, the pattern enables children to feel involved, whatever their age or level of attendance. Each session is designed to last approximately two hours, although this can be shortened or lengthened according to need. The book is packed with fresh suggestions for Bible stories, practical ideas for creating a display for the church, and a host of brand new craft activities, games and ideas for creative prayer. The material also includes an exciting summer activity programme based on the 'I am' sayings of Jesus.

Through-the-year themes include Baptism, Faith, Prayer, Miracles, Parables, Blessings, Forgiveness, Transfiguration, Jesus' friends, Jesus and me, and God with us.

ISBN 978 1 84101 578 1   £9.99
Available from your local Christian bookshop or, in case of difficulty, direct from BRF: please visit www.barnabasinchurches.org.uk.

Enjoyed
this book?

Write a review—we'd love to hear what you think.
Email: reviews@brf.org.uk

Keep up to date—receive details of our new books as they happen.
Sign up for email news and select your interest groups at:
www.brfonline.org.uk/findoutmore/

Follow us on Twitter @brfonline

By post—to receive new title information by post (UK only), complete the form below and post to: BRF Mailing Lists, 15 The Chambers, Vineyard, Abingdon, Oxfordshire, OX14 3FE

Your Details
Name _____
Address_____
_____
Town/City _____ Post Code _____
Email _____

Your Interest Groups (*Please tick as appropriate)	
☐ Advent/Lent	☐ Messy Church
☐ Bible Reading & Study	☐ Pastoral
☐ Children's Books	☐ Prayer & Spirituality
☐ Discipleship	☐ Resources for Children's Church
☐ Leadership	☐ Resources for Schools

Support your local bookshop
Ask about their new title information schemes.